THE NATIONAL PARKS OF CANADA

The NATIONAL PARKS of CANADA

Foreword by **DAVID SUZUKI**

Principal Photography by **J.A. KRAULIS**

Text by **KEVIN McNAMEE**

KEY PORTER BOOKS

To the late Robert Graham (1942–1993)

His dedication to conserving Canada's marine environment and to the

educational value of national parks will be sorely missed.

The author wishes to thank the many dedicated employees of Parks Canada who reviewed and offered suggestions on the park descriptions; the staff of Key Porter Books and Jacinthe Séguin for their editorial support; J. David Henry for giving me my first chance to lobby for national parks; and Bob Peart and John Theberge for making sure I made the most of it.

The publisher gratefully acknowledges the assistance of the Canada Council and the Ontario Arts Council.

Design: Scott Richardson • Typesetting: MacTrix DTP

Text copyright © 1994, 1998 Kevin McNamee
Photographs copyright © 1994, 1998 J.A. Kraulis

Canadian Cataloguing in Publication Data
McNamee, Kevin Alfred
The national parks of Canada
ISBN 1–55013–985-1
1. National parks and reserves – Canada – History.
I. Kraulis, J.A. II. Title.
FC215.M36 1998   333.78'3'0971
C98–095555–2
F1011.M36 1998

Key Porter Books Limited
70 The Esplanade, Toronto, Ontario
Canada M5E 1R2

Printed and bound in Hong Kong

98 99 00 01 6 5 4 3 2 1

3 9082 07433 0328

Page 1:
An exquisite clump of red maple signals the passing of another summer in Kouchibouguac National Park.

Page 2:
The slopes of Mount Athabasca and Mount Andromeda are bathed in morning light in Jasper National Park.

Page 3:
Late afternoon at the grassy flats and lagoon near Kelly's Beach in Kouchibouguac National Park. The Barrier Islands are visible offshore in Northumberland Strait.

Page 5:
Clear Lake is the largest lake in ecologically isolated Riding Mountain National Park.

Page 8:
The beauty of the forest in autumn masks the fact that La Mauricie is one of the most ecologically isolated national parks in Canada.

Pages 10 / 11:
Mountain peaks tower over Poboktan Creek in the back-country wilderness of Jasper National Park.

C O N T

E N T S

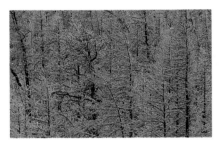

FOREWORD

David Suzuki

FOR 99 PERCENT OF OUR SPECIES' EXISTENCE, WE LIVED IN A STATE OF nature, as nomadic hunter-gatherers. We were totally immersed in, and dependent upon the abundance of our surroundings. Our situation has changed with astonishing speed. Three factors characterize this moment in history: the explosive growth of the human population; the even more dramatic development of modern technology; and the movement away from the land and into cities. Taken together, these factors have led to a rate of resource consumption so high that it is now straining the regenerative capacities of the earth.

The most unexpected consequence of the rise of cities is that most people now live in a human-created environment in which the connections with the natural world have become invisible. The economic system which now governs the way we live defines air, water, soil and biodiversity as *externalities*, thereby rendering the underpinnings of life itself as apparently irrelevant to our comfort and security. In cities, generations of children are growing up who are entirely unaware that everything they eat was once living, and that nature itself is the source of electricity, the origin of tapwater, and the final destination of garbage and sewage.

It is our disconnection from the natural world that has made us insensitive to the speed and magnitude of change that has happened on our planet. Lacking any direct contact with wild things and intact ecosystems, we live with the illusion that our science and technology give us the power to understand the world around us and to "manage" natural resources.

Our Common Future, the report by the commission chaired by Gro Harlem Brundtland, recommended that all nations preserve 12 percent of their terrestrial wilderness. Even though Canada is a vast country with a sparse population, we come nowhere near achieving that target either nationally or in any single province. Yet the Brundtland target assumes that 88 percent of all land is up for grabs by our species alone! At best, the target of 12 percent gives us a goal to aim at.

As the opportunity for individual citizens to experience nature diminishes, Canada's park system becomes a priceless treasure for all future generations. For scientists, intact wilderness offers the only opportunity to understand how complex ecosystems work. And for all Canadians, parks provide the opportunity to renew a physical bond and spiritual connection that is vital to our own and the earth's survival.

THE CANADIAN EXPERIENCE

"Three hundred years from now, these parks . . . will still be there. Nobody will remember me. Nobody.

But they will know the government did well to preserve this beautiful scenery."

— HON. JEAN CHRÉTIEN, MINISTER RESPONSIBLE FOR NATIONAL PARKS, 1968–1974

Sunset over Kejimkujik Lake.

Page 12:

Boulders and Mary Ann Falls, Cape Breton

Highlands National Park.

FROM ITS HUMBLE BEGINNINGS IN 1885, CANADA'S NATIONAL PARK SYSTEM HAS grown to thirty-eight national parks and national park reserves, protecting over 223,000 square kilometres (85,000 square miles) of the Canadian landscape in all provinces and territories. And there are plans to establish at least fifteen more national parks, preserving an additional 100,000 square kilometres (40,000 square miles). By the year 2000, a national park system half the size of the province of Alberta should be in place.

For over a century Canadians have flocked to these sanctuaries of nature to revel in their scenic grandeur. But national parks are more than a respite from industrial society. They are among the oldest conservation tools available. National parks are an important part of the nation's environmental agenda.

Our national parks – together with our extensive system of provincial parks – protect natural areas that are characteristic of the mosaic of land and seascapes that are the physical essence of Canada. In them we can glimpse the peaks of the Rocky Mountains that thrust skyward, the arctic tundra that seems endless, the ancient trees of the Pacific rainforest that tower over the coastline, the waves of the Atlantic ocean that crash against the fog-bound shores of Cape Breton, and the smooth outcrops of the Canadian Shield that were scoured by glaciers thousands of years ago. We can hear the call of wildlife that has come to symbolize our nation: the cry of the loon, the honking of Canada geese, and the bugling of elk and moose.

This book is a celebration of Canada's national parks and all the resplendent natural areas and wildlife they protect. It is a testament to the vision of the many Canadians who have worked since 1885 to conserve some of our nation's spectacular wilderness landscapes. It is meant to inspire Canadians to encourage and work for the expansion of the current national park system, and to pass it unimpaired to future generations so that they, too, may enjoy and protect Canada's natural heritage.

We have much to celebrate. Almost one-quarter of our national parks are recognized by the United Nations for their outstanding global conservation value. The Canadian Rocky Mountain Parks, along with Nahanni, Kluane, Gros Morne, Waterton Lakes, and Wood Buffalo national parks, are all designated World Heritage Sites under the World Heritage Convention, joining such famous places as the Grand Canyon, the Galapagos Islands, the Serengeti, the Great Barrier Reef, and Mount Everest.

Wetland habitats in Wood Buffalo, Vuntut, and Point Pelee national parks are recognized under an international convention signed in Ramsar, Iran, in 1971, as wetlands of international importance and high biological productivity. Riding Mountain, Waterton Lakes, and Bruce Peninsula national parks are part of an international network of over 300 biosphere reserves that represent the world's major ecological systems. Biosphere reserves are model conservation projects that demonstrate ways in which a protected core of relatively undisturbed lands can survive within a broader landscape that supports a range of human activities.

The need to spare selected natural areas from industrial exploitation has struck a resonant chord with Canadians for many years. At a time when the ecological survival of the planet is in doubt, national parks remain islands of hope. Through them, we can rediscover our essential connections to the natural world.

In 1930 the Canadian Parliament passed the *National Parks Act*, which states, "The National Parks of Canada are hereby dedicated to the people of Canada for their benefit, education and enjoyment," and they "shall be maintained and made use of so as to leave them unimpaired for the enjoyment of future generations." Parliament, however, did not define such words as "benefit" and "use." Consequently, different interest groups have given different meanings to these words. The *Act* has been interpreted variously to stress preservation of wilderness areas and wildlife habitats; provision of recreational opportunities; construction of tourism facilities such as hotels and roads; promotion of regional development through tourism; protection of natural resources used by aboriginal people and others who live off the land; protection of spectacular scenery; and simply the rescue of natural areas for their own intrinsic worth.

When a national park is created, the land itself is not altered, only human attitudes toward it. Park land is no longer a source of profit from the exploitation of timber, minerals, oil, and gas, or hydroelectric power. Instead, national parks are managed to ensure the preservation of their natural values, and to provide visitors with opportunities to experience their inspirational qualities. The *National Parks Act* forbids logging, mining, oil and gas development, and recreational hunting, so that the ecological, recreational, educational, and spiritual value of relatively pristine natural areas is retained for the benefit of present and future generations.

Under the *National Parks Act*, the Canadian Parliament has a legal obligation to pass on national parks to future generations. This is made possible by the fact that national park boundaries are protected under the *Act*. If the government wants to alter, or even delete, an existing national park, it must first table a bill and allow public debate in Parliament. Chances are, such legislation would never pass, or even see the light of day, given the strong level of public and political support for national park values.

The federal government neither establishes nor manages national parks for the financial benefit of one segment of society, or group of individuals. When a national park is established, a natural area is withdrawn from industrial development and held in trust by the government to ensure such natural areas benefit all species, not just humans. Priority is placed on protecting for all time the "ecological services" that are fundamental to sustaining life on the planet. These include healthy habitat, clean air and water, and a complete range of plant and animal species that are food sources for other species.

Conservation groups such as the Canadian Nature Federation, Canadian Parks and Wilderness Society, and World Wildlife Fund advocate the establishment of new national parks as an affirmation by Parliament, on behalf of the people of Canada, of the intrinsic value of natural areas. The existence of national parks also lends validity to the idea that Canada's land and waters are of value even when they are not developed into marketable products. When Parliament acts to keep thousands of square kilometres of wild land free of development, it sends a powerful message to Canadians that we must place a greater priority on conserving nature's life-sustaining processes.

Because there are no roads, canoeing may be the most efficient, as well as the most popular, way to get around Nahanni National Park Reserve.

Canadian ecologist Stan Rowe observed that "Countries that count themselves civilized need the symbolism of wild places to remind them of their sources and, in a deep way, of their continued co-existence in the world." Through our national park system, Canada has protected a number of landscapes that remind visitors of our origins, such as the temperate rainforest, boreal ecosystems, wild rivers, and the prairie grasslands. They remind us that it is natural areas such as these that produce and sustain sources of clean air and water, healthy wildlife, and vibrant ecosystems. But the extent to which we have succeeded in using national parks to remind Canadians of our dependence on the natural world remains to be seen. The fact that we have preserved only 6 percent of Canada in a wilderness state free of logging, mining, and hydroelectric development suggests we still have work to do.

PRESERVING OUR NATURAL INHERITANCE

The planet is threatened by a number of environmental crises. Solutions to global warming, ozone depletion, and population growth are difficult, elusive, and demand international cooperation. But the loss of biological diversity through the extinction of plant and animal species and the destruction of habitats is almost totally irreversible. When a species is lost, it's gone forever. It is also a crisis that requires domestic action by each nation. Despite the fact that they are the ecological and economic foundation of the human species and society, we continue to alter, exploit, and destroy the natural habitats that sustain life.

Most Canadians and their political leaders still believe that, in order to maintain a strong economy, we must continue to develop our natural resources. Calls for new wilderness reserves often bring the notions of wilderness preservation and resource development into conflict. But conflict over the use of wild places such as Clayoquot Sound and the growing scarcity of undisturbed wilderness areas continue to force us to reexamine our attitude toward our natural environment.

Canada is implicated in the loss of habitat and species. Reduced to remnants are Ontario's Carolinian forests and the prairie grasslands. Rare are the red- and white-pine old-growth forests of central Canada. Threatened are the old-growth spruce and cedar forests of western Canada, and almost gone are the hardwood forests of Atlantic Canada. The decline in species that inhabit these wild places reflects the loss of habitats. More than 270 plants and animals are listed as endangered, threatened, or rare. The Labrador duck and the great auk of the North Atlantic are already extinct. The future for grizzly bears, cougars, and wolves, along with piping plovers and Eskimo curlews, is questionable because of continuing habitat loss.

Canada possesses almost 20 percent of the world's remaining wilderness (excluding Antarctica). Like the people of the Amazon, we, too, have a rainforest with an incredible diversity of plants and animals. And like Africa's inhabitants, we, too, have great herds of wild animals whose migrations are a spectacle to behold. Caribou migrate across the arctic tundra by the thousands. Grizzly and black bears stake out their turf in the mountains and boreal forest. Remnant herds of buffalo still thunder across the northern plains. Whales chart their course through the waters of the Pacific, Atlantic, and Arctic oceans. Polar bears, seals, and narwhals gather in Lancaster Sound. Birds and butterflies fill the skies over Point Pelee.

The World Commission on Environment and Development (commonly known as the Brundtland Commission) called on all nations in its 1987 report, *Our Common Future*, to place the issue of disappearing species and threatened ecosystems on the political agenda. The Commission urged all countries to protect their species and ecosystems as a prerequisite to sustainable development. It recommended that each nation complete a network of strictly protected areas, including national parks, that represent each of the earth's major ecosystems as part of a global conservation strategy.

There is a growing international consensus that national parks and other protected areas play a critical role in sustaining life. Canada's national parks help stem the continuing loss of species and ecosystems. Representative examples of the endangered Carolinian forest and prairie grassland ecosystems are protected in Point Pelee and Grasslands national parks respectively, protecting the material that will allow us to restore these remnant ecosystems. Portions of the disappearing temperate rainforests are conserved in Gwaii Haanas and Pacific Rim national parks, while the threatened aspen parkland ecosystem is partially protected in Elk Island and Prince Albert national parks.

The critical calving grounds of the Porcupine caribou herd are preserved from oil and gas development in Ivvavik National Park in the northern Yukon. Wood Buffalo National Park contains the only known nesting ground of the threatened whooping crane. The only fully protected nesting colony of white pelican is in Prince Albert National Park. The endangered peregrine falcon has been reintroduced in Fundy National Park, and a habitat for the endangered piping plover is conserved in several maritime national parks including Prince Edward Island National Park.

National parks are like the canary in the mine shaft: they indicate when commercial and industrial activity has gone too far. By monitoring the ecological health of these relatively pristine natural areas, we can identify those human activities that are affecting the natural environment. The impact of acid rain on natural ecosystems, for example, is monitored in Kejimkujik National Park. Prince Albert National Park is part of a network of monitoring stations tracking the ecological changes caused by global climate change. And the quality of water in Nahanni National Park Reserve is under observation because several mine sites outside the park may be developed in the near future.

Since the release of the Brundtland Commission's report, the federal government has taken several steps to improve the contribution of Canada's national park system to conservation. Parliament amended the *National Parks Act* in 1988 to make the maintenance of ecological integrity through the protection of natural resources the first priority in managing parkland. In 1990, it made a commitment to establish eighteen more national parks by the year 2000. And in November, 1992, the ministers of parks, environment, and wildlife from the federal, provincial, and territorial governments committed to completing Canada's network of protected areas by the year 2000.

But it is not enough simply to establish more national parks. Our ecological future cannot be guaranteed by designating 5, 10, or 15 percent of Canada as protected space and allowing the rest to be fully exploited. In its report, *A Protected Areas Vision for Canada*, the Canadian Environmental Advisory Council stated that if national parks and protected areas "do not inform and inspire society to apply a land ethic in all human activities, they fail in their essential mission." Thus, national parks must become "catalysts for the improved management of human activities in all parts of Canada."

Origins of the National Park Idea

The creation of national parks, according to Parks Canada ecologist Stephen Woodley, is a societal response to ecosystem decay. In a perfect world, we would not need national parks because society would instinctively protect undisturbed wild lands. But this is not a perfect world: wild places are lost to development every day because we are simply ignorant of, or choose to ignore, the need to conserve them.

It was the deterioration of the prairie environment that first prompted the idea for a national park. The American landscape painter George Catlin called for "a great government policy of protection" to save the buffalo and its

An arctic sunset near the top of the world —
Ellesmere Island National Park Reserve.

habitat, and the Indians who depended on them, from extinction. He wrote in 1832, "What a beautiful and thrilling specimen for America to preserve and hold up to the view of her refined citizens and the world, in future ages! A nation's park, containing man and beast, in all the wild and freshness of their nature's beauty!" It was some time before Catlin's idea bore fruit.

The U.S. federal government was urged in February 1864 to obtain ownership of the Yosemite Valley in California and the giant sequoia trees in Mariposa Grove. Israel Raymond Ward, an employee of a steamship company, wanted the areas saved from occupation by settlers "to preserve the trees in the valley from destruction." Ward did not want to exclude people from Yosemite, but he did not want to see it settled by people who would destroy it. He recommended that Yosemite be placed in public ownership, and that the area be set aside "for public use, resort, and recreation." He also urged that the grant be made "inalienable forever," and the area "preserved for the benefit of mankind." President Abraham Lincoln signed the *Yosemite Park Act* in 1864. The *Act* withdrew the area from private settlement so as to preserve in the national interest Yosemite's stunning natural scenery.

The original intent of the *Yosemite Park Act* was to transfer the area to the state of California. But the state refused to keep Yosemite free of private settlement and sought to uphold the claims of two individuals who had settled in the Yosemite Valley. The U.S. Senate refused to recognize the claims, and the intent of the *Yosemite Park Act*, to preserve this remarkable place free of private ownership, was upheld in the nation's interest. So, despite its early beginnings, almost a quarter of a century passed before the area was designated Yosemite National Park, in 1890.

The first "nation's park" was established in the United States when Congress created Yellowstone National Park in 1872. Catlin's idea for a grasslands national park would not be realized for another 150 years when the government of Canada created Grasslands National Park in Saskatchewan. Catlin's related idea, about the survival of native people through the conservation of land and wildlife, was for the time being lost. Again, it took a century and a half before the role of native people and wildlife was reconciled within a "nation's park." The Canadian Parliament created Ivvavik National Park in 1984 at the request of the Inuvialuit of the western Arctic to protect the Porcupine caribou herd and its calving grounds in the northern Yukon. Parliament guaranteed the role of native people in co-managing this resource.

Today, over 120 nations have established more than 1,000 national parks. The benefits that accrue to society from national parks have been more broadly defined over the years, but the idea behind national parks remains the same: preserving natural areas from industrial development for the benefit of present and future generations.

BUILD IT, AND THEY SHALL COME (1885-1911)

On a cool November day in 1883 three employees of the Canadian Pacific Railway (CPR) pushed away the fallen timber from a large pool of steaming water that smelled of sulphur. Climbing up a bank, they found an opening in the ground that vented steam and a gurgling sound. Franklin McCabe of Nova Scotia, and brothers William and Thomas McCardell of Perth County, Ontario, had discovered several mineral hot springs in the Bow Valley of the Rocky Mountains.

They promptly applied to the federal government for private ownership of the springs. Their request drew the attention of the government and the CPR. After visiting the site, the head of the CPR, William Cornelius Van Horne, declared: "These springs are worth a million dollars!" Even for the times this was probably a modest valuation of the future Banff National Park.

The federal government rejected the application, and created a

26-square-kilometre (10-square-mile) reserve around the hot springs in November 1885, saving them from "sale, or settlement, or squatting." The cabinet order protecting the hot springs clearly reflected their value to the government: "There have been discovered several hot mineral springs which promise to be of great sanitary advantage to the public." The foundation for Canada's national park system was described in 1885 as nothing more than a giant spa. The government of Prime Minister Sir John A. Macdonald set out to make the Banff hot springs "the greatest and most successful health resort on the continent." In 1886 it called for a plan "to commence the construction of roads and bridges and other operations to make of the reserve a creditable National Park."

The reserve was quickly expanded. A government surveyor found "a large tract of country lying outside of the original reservation" with "features of the greatest beauty" that "were admirably adapted for a national park." Parliament acted on the surveyor's find, and passed the *Rocky Mountain Park Act* in 1887 to enlarge the reservation to 675 square kilometres (270 square miles). The *Act* stated that Rocky Mountain Park (it was renamed Banff National Park in 1930) was "a public park and pleasuring ground for the benefit, advantage and enjoyment" of Canadians. The language used was similar to legislation creating Yellowstone National Park, which was created "as a public park or pleasuring ground for the benefit and enjoyment of the people."

The new park reserve had nothing to do with wilderness protection. In the mid-to-late 1800s, there was no need to protect wilderness – it seemed plentiful. In fact, wilderness then was a resource to conquer and exploit. The national purpose from the time the first settlers arrived was to subdue this massive continent, including its original native inhabitants, and to remake it in the image of the European settlers. Fur traders, lumberjacks, mineral explorers, and other men of commerce set about exploiting the trees, wildlife, minerals, and waters, laying waste to the natural beauty about them.

The exploitation of western Canada became a dominant federal policy with the election of Sir John A. Macdonald as prime minister in 1878. Macdonald's National Policy called for the development of the region's natural resources, and the new transcontinental railway was the key to it. The creation of Rocky Mountain Park, along with two additional reserves in 1886 along the line of the transcontinental railway – Glacier and Yoho – was simply an extension of the National Policy. The government and the CPR believed that if appropriate accommodation was provided, people would pay to experience what nature, and the CPR , had to offer: mineral hot springs, mountain scenery, the transcontinental railway, and luxurious accommodation in the mountains.

In short, national parks were yet another resource to be exploited. To this end, the CPR built the Banff Springs Hotel, Mount Stephen House, and Glacier Park Lodge in the Banff, Yoho, and Glacier reserves. The government of the day felt it was on the right track. As one civil servant wrote: "The efforts of the Government of Canada to establish a health and pleasure resort in the heart of the Rocky Mountains . . . have been so warmly appreciated and so largely taken advantage of."

Logging, mining, grazing, and hunting were also permitted in the new parks early in their history. Lead, zinc, and silver were mined from Yoho National Park. In Rocky Mountain Park, the towns of Bankhead and Anthracite were built to extract coal. The superintendent of Rocky Mountain did not consider Bankhead to be "a detriment to the beauty of the park." It was a welcome addition, and with its "teeming industrial life," "a popular stopping place for tourists." Only a few politicians raised objections to such developments. One member of Parliament told Macdonald: "You cannot have a public park, with all the wild animals preserved in it, and have mining industries going

A lighthouse facility is still maintained in Mingan Archipelago National Park Reserve.

on at the same time. . . . If you intend to keep it as a park, you must shut out trade, traffic, and mining." But his was a voice lost in the political wilderness.

As the national transportation systems opened Canada to more development and tourism, the historical rejection of the value of wilderness slowly dissipated. It was replaced by what historian George Woodcock called "a mystique of the land, a desire to cherish and understand what had once seemed entirely impenetrable." The CPR played an important role in promoting this mystique. Landscape painters such as John A. Fraser and Lucius O'Brien were hired by the CPR to paint the great natural wonders of the Rocky Mountains. Their paintings, along with the photographs of Byron Harmon, brought the spectacular scenery of the Canadian Rockies to world attention, and helped to develop a more romantic view of the Canadian wilderness.

While the profit motive gave birth to the national park idea in Canada, the need to conserve natural areas gradually gained acceptance. In 1893, an Alberta rancher asked the federal government to create a park in the Waterton Lakes area to protect it from settlement. Two years later Waterton Lakes Forest Park, later named Waterton Lakes National Park, was created. The decision to proceed with the Waterton park was an important watershed. Some government officials felt that creating Waterton was overdoing the business of national parks. Deputy minister A.M. Burgess advised the minister in charge of the parks accordingly: "It would be far better to have only one or two parks at important points, and to have them faithfully and well protected, than a larger number of reservations none of which the public would regard." The Honourable T.M. Daly ignored the advice and directed officials to proceed with the park, remarking that "posterity will bless us."

Looking back after a century, we can only conclude that Canadians have indeed been blessed by the farsighted decisions of politicians like Macdonald and Daly. The first parks were, in effect, islands of civilization in a sea of wilderness. It would be up to future generations, who grew to appreciate the need to protect wilderness areas in a world of declining resources, to redefine the national parks mandate. But at least we had a legacy to redefine for conservation purposes.

BRINGING THE NATIONAL PARKS TO CANADIANS (1911-1960)

The loose collection of national parks that existed in 1911 were a vulnerable lot. Passage of the *Dominion Forest Reserves and Parks Act* by Parliament in 1911 underscored their vulnerability to political manipulation. The legislation substantially reduced the size of Rocky Mountain Park, Jasper, and Waterton Lakes national parks. For example, Jasper was reduced from 13,000 (5,200) to 2,600 square kilometres (1,040 square miles).

But the federal government unwittingly planted the seeds for later reversal. The Dominion Parks Branch (now called Parks Canada) was created in 1911, predating the U.S. National Parks Service by two years, making it the world's first government agency responsible solely for administering national parks. The national park idea benefited greatly from the gentleman appointed to be the first commissioner of the National Parks Branch – James Bernard Harkin. Among his first achievements was a re-enlargement of these parks. Jasper, for example, was enlarged to 10,400 square kilometres (4,160 square miles), which it has remained to this date.

Harkin brought to the job a mystical reverence for wilderness along with a pragmatic view of its economic value. He wrote that national parks were created so that "every citizen of Canada may satisfy his soul-craving for nature." He believed that national parks protect "some of the finest scenery in Canada" and retain "the peace and solitude of primeval nature." Harkin worked from 1911 to 1930 to exclude industrial development in national parks. He achieved his goal in 1930 when Parliament passed the *National Parks Act*, which

prohibits logging, mining, oil and gas exploration, and recreational hunting inside park boundaries.

Harkin also advocated the protection of more wilderness lands: "Future generations may wonder at our blindness if we neglect to set them aside before civilization invades them." During Harkin's tenure, the system was expanded from its base of five national parks in the Rocky Mountains to eighteen national parks protecting over 31,000 square kilometres (12,400 square miles), including the first parks in Saskatchewan (Prince Albert), Manitoba (Riding Mountain), Ontario (Point Pelee, Georgian Bay, and St. Lawrence Islands), and Nova Scotia (Cape Breton Highlands).

Some of the new parks focused on conservation. Elk Island National Park was created in 1913 to prevent the elimination of elk herds. Wood Buffalo was established in 1922 to protect the only remaining herd of wood buffalo in its wild state. On Harkin's recommendation, the federal government also created the Nemiskan, Wawakesy, and Menissawok national parks in 1922 to conserve the prong-horned antelope, which were in danger of extinction on the western prairie. This emphasis on conservation occurred because there was growing concern about the loss of wildlife to over-hunting, and about fires started by the railway that destroyed valuable timber. Species such as buffalo, elk, and antelope were on the verge of extinction.

To secure the necessary financing from Parliament to expand and administer the national parks system, Harkin aggressively promoted the tourism value of national parks. Calculating the value of national parks to be $300 million dollars in 1922, he concluded, "I don't think there is an institution in Canada that pays as big a dividend as the Canadian National Parks." He told Parliament that "National Parks provide the chief means of bringing to Canada a stream of tourists and streams of tourist gold." By 1916 a wider use of automobiles was permitted in the national parks. Harkin exclaimed: "What a revenue this country will obtain when thousands of autos are traversing the parks." More visitor accommodation was provided, minor attractions to supplement natural features were built, and first class roads were constructed.

Harkin was well aware of the thin line between use and protection in national parks. But he believed that the parks belonged to Canadians, that they had a right to use them. "It is the duty of those in charge to make them freely accessible by road and trail, and to permit under the regulation the provision of accommodation, refreshments and other needs. But the more the parks are used, the more difficult it is to prevent abuse. . . . The parks may lose the very thing that distinguished them from the outside world." This dual mandate, to use and protect, was enshrined in the *National Parks Act* that Harkin helped to formulate. It states that the national parks "shall be maintained and made use of so as to leave them unimpaired for the enjoyment of future generations."

Some still point to the *National Parks Act* as justification for development. However, they fail to examine the issue in its proper context. Harkin felt that by allowing development he would gain political support for expanding the system. This policy produced new national parks that might never have been created otherwise. But to continue to focus on tourism development in the 1990s risks making the national parks irrelevant to the international conservation agenda.

Years after retiring from the National Parks Branch, Harkin expressed his disappointment at the lack of a public constituency to defend the parks: "What is needed in Canada today is an informed public opinion which will voice an indignant protest against any vulgarization of the beauty of our National Parks or any invasion of their sanctity." There was no organization of citizens to watch over the national parks in Canada as there was in the United States. Consequently, the federal government was able to eliminate

Nemiskan, Wawakesy, and Menissawok national parks in 1947 without opposition. That same year the size of Waterton Lakes and Prince Albert national parks was reduced. Lands were removed subsequently from Cape Breton Highlands for mineral and hydro development, and logging was permitted in Wood Buffalo National Park.

An earlier attempt to form an advocacy group had floundered. In 1923 the National Parks Association of Canada was formed to lobby against plans by the Calgary Power Corporation to dam the Spray River near Canmore, Alberta, which at that time was inside Rocky Mountain Park. The issue was lost, however, when the government amended the boundaries of Rocky Mountain Park in 1930 to eliminate the Kananaskis and Spray river valleys. These two rivers were eventually dammed, and the Association disappeared. But the rise of the National Parks Association, for however short a time, set an important precedent for later groups.

DEFENDING THE NATIONAL PARKS (1960 TO 1985)

Speaking to a national conference in Banff National Park in 1968, wilderness historian Roderick Nash suggested that the "Canadian public's sensitivity to and enthusiasm for wilderness lags at least two generations behind opinion in the United States." Canadians, he said, still regarded themselves as a pioneering people with an overabundance of wild country. We had no environmental milestones similar to those in the United States, such as the fight to stop the Grand Canyon from being dammed or passage of the U.S. *Wilderness Act* of 1964, which made wilderness protection a national goal. These issues galvanized the American public into fighting to preserve wild areas. Nothing similar had galvanized Canadians.

Even as Nash spoke, the situation had already started to change. In 1960, national parks minister Alvin Hamilton decried the lack of an association to promote the preservation of "those beautiful scenic areas of the country." He asked the House of Commons: "How can a minister stand up against the pressures of commercial interests who want to use the parks for mining, forestry, for every kind of honky-tonk device known to man, unless the people who love these parks are prepared to band together and support the minister by getting the facts out across the country?" Several Canadians responded to Hamilton's call and in 1963 formed the National and Provincial Parks Association of Canada (NPPAC), now the Canadian Parks and Wilderness Society.

Other groups, such as the Alberta Wilderness Association and the Algonquin Wildlands League, were formed to defend the Canadian wilderness. The growth in these groups in the 1960s was prompted by the meteoric rise of an environmental consciousness among Canadians and Americans, prompted in part by the publication of Rachel Carson's powerful book *Silent Spring*. They were inspired, too, by what Dr. Robert Page of the University of Calgary called "a literature of protest against the development ethic implicit in the evolution of Canada," as exemplified in the novels of Margaret Atwood and Wayland Drew.

The NPPAC scored some impressive early victories in defense of park values. In 1964 it got the government to release its first national parks policy, which had sat in draft form on the shelf for several years. The policy provided continuity in the management of national parks that would extend beyond the term of each government. Government was compelled under the policy to make the preservation of significant natural features in national parks the "most fundamental and important obligation." The new policy also put an end to any further industrial activity in areas that had been allocated to industry prior to passage of the *National Parks Act*. In essence, this was a new contract between the federal government and Canadians that elaborated the terms under which the government maintained the public trust in the national parks.

The NPPAC also led a successful national battle to defeat a proposed multimillion-dollar tourism development in Banff National Park called Village Lake Louise. This battle helped to make the point that increasing tourism in national parks would compromise their wilderness character. The level of development within Banff remains high, but it is much lower in other parks. In the battle over Village Lake Louise, the government was also forced to hold public hearings. Until then, government decisions were not subjected to public debate.

Doubling the Size of Canada's National Park System

At the formal opening of Kejimkujik National Park in 1969, the president of the NPPAC, Al Frame, bet the Hon. Jean Chrétien he couldn't establish nine new national parks in five years. The growth in environmental advocacy groups in support of national park expansion, coupled with strong public support for environmental protection, helped the minister to win the bet. Riding this wave of support, Chrétien, the federal minister responsible for national parks from 1968 to 1974, established an unprecedented ten new national parks totalling almost 53,000 square kilometres (21,200 square miles), doubling the size of the national park system.

Chrétien had wanted to establish forty to sixty new national parks to represent Canada's major landscapes by the year 2000. He envisaged five to ten in the province of Quebec because, at that time, there were no national parks in his home province. Chrétien told a meeting of the Gaspé Chamber of Commerce that a park would stimulate the local tourism industry by providing an incentive for visitors to remain longer in the area. His arguments were convincing. In 1970, the federal government and Quebec reached an agreement creating Forillon National Park. Chrétien also succeeded in establishing La Mauricie National Park in his own constituency of Saint-Maurice.

Chrétien was successful in filling another gap in the national parks system – northern Canada. In 1972, the federal government announced the creation of three new national parks: Kluane, Nahanni, and Auyuittuq. Chrétien was proud of his action: "I made the decision that there will never be mineral development in the spectacular landscape of Kluane National Park, just as Virginia Falls on the South Nahanni River will never be the site of a hydroelectric development."

His other accomplishments included the establishment of the first new national park in British Columbia in over four decades; an agreement with the Ontario government that produced Pukaskwa as Ontario's first large national park; and three major new national parks in the maritime provinces. Chrétien later remarked that "three hundred years from now these parks … will still be there. Nobody will remember me. Nobody. But they will know the government did well to preserve this beautiful scenery."

There were, however, several unexpected sources of opposition to the expansion of the national park system. And this opposition provoked a number of significant changes to the process by which national parks are made. The first emerged when legislation was introduced into Parliament in 1973 to formally protect Kluane, Nahanni, and Auyuittuq under the *National Parks Act*. Native leaders from the Yukon and the Northwest Territories expressed strong opposition. Because of the threat mining and hydroelectric development posed to their traditional homelands, this opposition was not expected by conservation interests. However, there was a larger principle at play.

The Liberal government of Prime Minister Pierre Elliott Trudeau was preparing to negotiate land-claim agreements with native people in northern Canada who had never ceded title or any rights in the first place. In creating new parks, native leaders said, the government was bypassing the claims process and unilaterally taking land away from native people. The Inuit, for example, claimed ownership of the land that was proposed for Auyuittuq National Park on Baffin Island. They charged that this was a form of expropriation without compensation, and in violation of the Canadian Charter of Rights. Negotiations for other proposed national parks came to a halt because of the objections of native leaders. Plans for national parks to protect the Torngats and the Mealy Mountains in Labrador and the East Arm of Great Slave Lake ended because native leaders first wanted action on their broader claims.

A quick solution was found to the issue of Kluane, Nahanni, and Auyuittuq. The *National Parks Act* was amended to protect native rights by designating national parks in the Yukon and Northwest Territories as national park reserves. In essence, these areas are reserved for national park purposes pending the settlement of any aboriginal claims. The 1993 final land-claim agreement between the federal government and the Tungavik Federation of Nunavut provided for the final creation of Auyuittuq National Park. The *Act* was also amended to guarantee the inherent right of aboriginal people to continue to hunt, trap, and fish in northern national parks, which prior to 1974 was not permitted under the Act.

This principle is being applied in southern national parks. For example, Mingan Archipelago, Pacific Rim, and Gwaii Haanas in the South Moresby archipelago are all designated national park reserves. In 1993, the Haida and the government of Canada signed an historic agreement that guarantees the Haida a role as co-managers of the South Moresby area. The agreement outlines the divergent views of both parties on ownership in the absence of a land-claim agreement: the Haida see the South Moresby archipelago as Haida lands under the jurisdiction of the Haida House of Assembly while the government of Canada views the archipelago as Crown land, subject to the jurisdiction of Parliament. However, they both agree that they must work together "to safeguard the archipelago as one of the world's great natural and cultural treasures, and that the highest standards of protection and preservation should be applied."

Working through an Archipelago Management Board that has equal representation from the Haida and Parks Canada, both parties "agree that the Archipelago will be maintained and made use of so as to leave it unimpaired for the benefit, education, and enjoyment of future generations." These are words taken from the *National Parks Act* and ratified by both the Haida House of Assembly and Parliament. In short, the Haida and the government agree to disagree on who owns the land, but are willing to work together to preserve it in advance of a final land-claim settlement.

Local communities played a strong role in lobbying for some of Canada's early national parks. Numerous resolutions from city and town councils in 1927, for example, urged the creation of Riding Mountain National Park. However, local attitudes toward national parks began to change in the 1960s. Government policy was to expropriate privately held lands that were to become national parks and to compensate the owners for their loss. This was done because it was felt such communities would compromise the wilderness character of the lands the parks were supposed to protect. In addition, the government did not want to have to deal with any more communities like Banff that continued to grow inside a national park.

More than 200 families were removed from their land by the Quebec government to create Forillon National Park. And almost 1,200 residents and over 225 households were relocated to facilitate land acquisition for Kouchibouguac National Park. However, society was beginning to question and resist the intrusion of those who exercised authority over their lives in the late 1960s, and this began to manifest itself in protests against government plans for new parks. Local opposition completely halted plans for a national park in

Ship Harbour, Nova Scotia. And protests in the Kouchibouguac area resulted in the appointment of a commission of enquiry to review the situation.

In light of this experience, the federal government changed its policy. The power of expropriation is no longer used to remove people from proposed national parks; instead, the government purchases land only from willing sellers. This is the policy guiding land acquisition for the Grasslands and the Bruce Peninsula national parks. And in the case of Gros Morne, the park boundary was drawn around several communities, excluding them from the park. The *National Parks Act* was amended to allow people living in these communities to remove timber and snare rabbits for personal use.

Today, local communities are an integral part of the park establishment process. For example, the federal government had to resolve almost fifty issues identified by local people before the Ontario government agreed to the creation of the Bruce Peninsula National Park. The final boundaries were reduced by 25 percent after the people of Lindsay township voted against the park in a plebiscite in 1986. Elsewhere, representatives of local communities are at the negotiating table helping to define the impact and benefits of proposed national parks. For example, the community of Churchill worked with officials from Parks Canada and Manitoba to review possible park boundaries for Wapusk National Park, as well as arrangements to involve them in management, and economic incentives that may accrue to the community. While this makes park negotiations longer and more complicated, it ensures strong local support at the end of the process. This is essential for the long-term survival of national parks.

THE SECOND CENTURY (1985 TO THE PRESENT)

Plans to celebrate the 1985 centennial of Banff National Park were overshadowed by controversy and disappointment. No new national parks were created. Parks Canada's plans to obtain cabinet approval and financing to complete the national park system by the year 2000 were shelved. And the first environment minister under the newly elected Conservative government refused to rule out logging and mining in new national parks. The future of the national park system in its second century was looking dim.

Prospects improved when the Hon. Tom McMillan assumed the national parks portfolio in August 1985. He brought to the portfolio a new enthusiasm for national parks that produced some important gains between 1985 and 1988. He succeeded in finalizing negotiations, which had languished under previous ministers, to complete the Grasslands and Pacific Rim national parks. He also established Ellesmere Island as Canada's second-largest national park, and the Bruce Peninsula National Park. A new federal policy committing the federal government to creating national marine parks was approved in 1986. And the first major overhaul of the *National Parks Act* was completed, strengthening the government's ability to preserve the national parks from inappropriate development.

But it was McMillan's determination to preserve the temperate rainforest of the South Moresby archipelago on the Queen Charlotte Islands that distinguished his tenure as national parks minister. Since 1974 a small group of environmentalists and Haida had laboured to preserve this area from proposed clear-cut logging. The issue gained international prominence when seventy-two Haida were arrested in 1985 while blockading a logging road on Lyell Island. In July 1987, Canada and British Columbia signed a park agreement creating the Gwaii Haanas National Park Reserve (originally known as South Moresby National Park Reserve), putting an end to the logging that had started to destroy Lyell Island.

Gwaii Haanas was more than a victory for national park advocates and the Haida. It was the first of a number of issues that forced Canadians to come to grips with their shrinking wilderness heritage. The national campaign that followed the arrest of the Haida brought to the country's attention the plight of native people and ancient rainforests in Canada at a time when many were focusing on the Amazon rainforest. It also gave national attention to the disappearing wilderness lands of southern Canada. Battles such as that fought over South Moresby threaten to undermine our credibility on the international stage. How can Canadians urge the protection of the Amazon rainforest if we cannot save the rainforest in our own country?

Other wilderness battles have ensued. Over 120 people were arrested trying to prevent logging trucks from squirrelling away the last of the old-growth red and white pines of Temagami in 1988. Almost 70 people were arrested defending British Columbia's first provincial park, Strathcona, from proposed mineral exploration in 1989. And police arrested over 700 people in the bitter fight to save the Clayoquot Sound wilderness in 1993. More and more Canadians were responding to the call of environmental groups to sign petitions, write letters, and march in support of further wilderness gains. The World Wildlife Fund and Canadian Parks and Wilderness Society launched the Endangered Spaces campaign in 1989 for the purpose of translating growing public support for wilderness conservation into political action. The goal of the campaign is to get all thirteen major governments to complete their network of parks and protected areas by the year 2000.

The politicians were hearing these calls. The federal government was the first to endorse the campaign goal in 1989. Parliament passed a resolution in June 1991 calling on the federal government to work with the provinces and territories to help expand their networks of protected areas so that at least 12 percent of Canada would be preserved free of development. And in 1992, all the federal, provincial, and territorial ministers of parks, environment, and wildlife committed to representing each of the natural regions in their jurisdictions in a network of parks and protected areas.

Some solid conservation gains have been made since 1989. Four new national parks and national park reserves totalling over 46,000 square kilometres (16,000 square miles) were created in northern Canada. The British Columbia government created the Tatshenshini Provincial Wilderness Park to protect the international wilderness and wildlife values of this area in the province's northwestern corner. The park put an end to the proposed Windy Craggy open-pit copper mine opposed by environmentalists and the U.S. government. The province also created the country's first grizzly bear sanctuary in the Khutzeymateen Valley, and worked with the Haisla Nation to protect the largest tract of temperate rainforest in North America. The Newfoundland government created the Bay du Nord Wilderness Reserve. Nova Scotia set aside almost 20 percent of its Crown land in 31 new protected areas.

Canada is on an environmental threshold. Citizens are questioning the wisdom of a national economy in which economic growth largely precludes wilderness protection. And while Canada's first national parks were islands of civilization within a sea of wilderness, developed for tourism purposes, they are now islands of wilderness within a sea of development, and a key to conserving the Canadian landscape. While we have much to celebrate when we look at the photographs on the following pages, we need to look beyond the boundaries of national parks, to apply the same standard of care we lavish on parks to the rest of the landscape. Future generations of all living things depend on it.

La Chute is an especially picturesque waterfall in Forillon National Park.

1   **Ellesmere Island**
2   **Aulavik**
3   **Ivvavik**
4   **Vuntut**
5   **Kluane**
6   **Gwaii Haanas**
7   **Pacific Rim**
8   **Nahanni**
9   **Wood Buffalo**
10   **Jasper**
11   **Banff**
12   **Glacier**
13   **Mount Revelstoke**
14   **Yoho**
15   **Kootenay**
16   **Waterton Lakes**
17   **Grasslands**
18   **Prince Albert**
19   **Elk Island**
20   **Riding Mountain**
21   **North Baffin Island**
22   **Auyuittuq**
23   **Pukaskwa**
24   **Georgian Bay Islands**
25   **Bruce Peninsula**
26   **Point Pelee**
27   **St. Lawrence Islands**
28   **La Mauricie**
29   **Kouchibouguac**
30   **Fundy**
31   **Kejimkujik**
32   **Prince Edward Island**
33   **Forillon**
34   **Mingain Archipalego**
35   **Cape Breton Highlands**
36   **Gros Morne**
37   **Terra Nova**
38   **Wapusk**
39   **Tuktut Nogait**

The National Parks of Canada

WILDERNESS INHERITANCE

"Few nations have been so profoundly shaped by the forces of nature as Canada. Even today its people must habitually contend with the immutable facts of their environment — its overwhelming magnitude, its emptiness, its rough and savage terrain, and its extremes of climate. All have determined this country's struggle to survive under circumstances that seem unfit for urbanized man."

— DAVID WISTOW, *TOM THOMSON AND THE GROUP OF SEVEN* (TORONTO: ART GALLERY OF ONTARIO, 1982)

FROM SPACE WE HAVE SEEN THE EARTH AS A BRIGHT BUT FRAGILE BALL DOMINATED by patterns of clouds, ocean, and greenery. Upon closer inspection, we can distinguish some of the distinctive patterns of the Canadian landscape – Hudson Bay, the Gulf of St. Lawrence, Newfoundland, Vancouver Island, the Great Lakes, and the Arctic islands. Look even closer and you can observe physical differences between mountains, forests, prairies, and arctic ice. These features are the foundation of the national park system.

The map on page 33 shows the thirty-nine terrestrial regions that are the basis of Canada's park system. There are "observable differences" in the landforms and vegetation in each of these natural regions. The mountains and temperate rainforests of the west, the plains of the prairie grasslands, and the sand dunes and salt marshes of the Maritimes are all distinct natural regions. Each supports distinct plants and animals. All contribute to the incredible diversity of the land. The goal of Parks Canada, the federal agency that administers our national parks, is to protect for all time representative examples of each of these 39 major landscapes.

The photographs of Canada's national parks on the following pages are presented in the eight geographical zones illustrated in the map on the facing page. These zones have been developed simply to group the thirty-nine natural regions for descriptive purposes in this book. The information about the eight geographical zones has been drawn from the "National Parks System Plan" written by Max Finklestein of Parks Canada. Leaders can obtain this informative document free from the Park Establishment Branch, Parks Canada, 25 Eddy Street, Hull, Quebec, K1A 0M5.

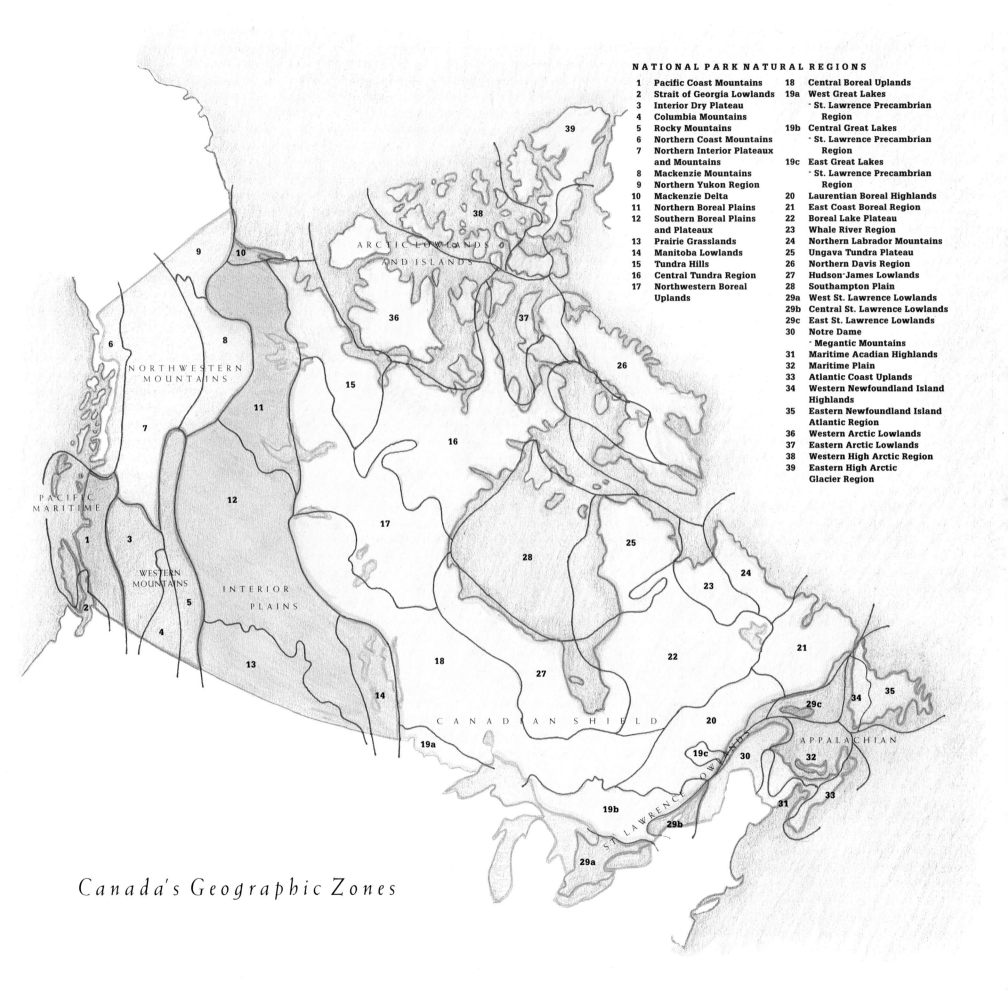

NATIONAL PARK NATURAL REGIONS

1 Pacific Coast Mountains
2 Strait of Georgia Lowlands
3 Interior Dry Plateau
4 Columbia Mountains
5 Rocky Mountains
6 Northern Coast Mountains
7 Northern Interior Plateaux and Mountains
8 Mackenzie Mountains
9 Northern Yukon Region
10 Mackenzie Delta
11 Northern Boreal Plains
12 Southern Boreal Plains and Plateaux
13 Prairie Grasslands
14 Manitoba Lowlands
15 Tundra Hills
16 Central Tundra Region
17 Northwestern Boreal Uplands
18 Central Boreal Uplands
19a West Great Lakes
    - St. Lawrence Precambrian Region
19b Central Great Lakes
    - St. Lawrence Precambrian Region
19c East Great Lakes
    - St. Lawrence Precambrian Region
20 Laurentian Boreal Highlands
21 East Coast Boreal Region
22 Boreal Lake Plateau
23 Whale River Region
24 Northern Labrador Mountains
25 Ungava Tundra Plateau
26 Northern Davis Region
27 Hudson-James Lowlands
28 Southampton Plain
29a West St. Lawrence Lowlands
29b Central St. Lawrence Lowlands
29c East St. Lawrence Lowlands
30 Notre Dame
    - Megantic Mountains
31 Maritime Acadian Highlands
32 Maritime Plain
33 Atlantic Coast Uplands
34 Western Newfoundland Island Highlands
35 Eastern Newfoundland Island Atlantic Region
36 Western Arctic Lowlands
37 Eastern Arctic Lowlands
38 Western High Arctic Region
39 Eastern High Arctic Glacier Region

Canada's Geographic Zones

THE PACIFIC MARITIME

THE TALL TREES OF THE ANCIENT TEMPERATE RAINFORESTS ARE AMONG THE most powerful physical features associated with the Pacific Maritime zone. Only about 0.2 percent of the planet is covered by temperate rainforest. Half of that stretches along the west coast of North America from northern California to Alaska. This forest has flourished undisturbed since the last ice age about 11,000 years ago. Over the last hundred years, however, the lush rainforests of the Queen Charlotte Islands, Vancouver Island, and mainland British Columbia have been dramatically reduced by axe and chainsaw.

The Pacific Maritime zone extends from southern Vancouver Island to the southern Alaskan border. The distinctive features of the Pacific Coast Mountains natural region are represented in the Gwaii Haanas National Park Reserve on the Queen Charlotte Islands and Pacific Rim National Park Reserve on the west coast of Vancouver Island. Parks Canada hopes to establish a national park in the Gulf Islands to represent the Strait of Georgia Lowlands natural region.

Standing on the shore of mainland British Columbia or Vancouver Island, you are witness to a tremendous diversity of life. Look to the ocean and there are the undersea forests of kelp, frolicking sea lions, seals, and the sleek-swimming, reintroduced sea otter. The Pacific surf pounds the rocky shore. The tides ebb and flow in countless fiords that are among the world's longest and deepest.

Turn inland and you enter the ancient temperate rainforest that stretches along the coast. These forests are composed of red and yellow cedar, hemlock, mountain hemlock, Douglas fir, and Sitka spruce. Moderate temperatures and heavy rainfall make these the most productive forests in Canada. They are characterized by landmark trees such as 85-metre (280-foot) Douglas fir trees in Cathedral Grove; the tallest – 95-metre (315-foot) – Sitka spruce, in Carmanah Valley; and the largest western cedar, with a 20-metre

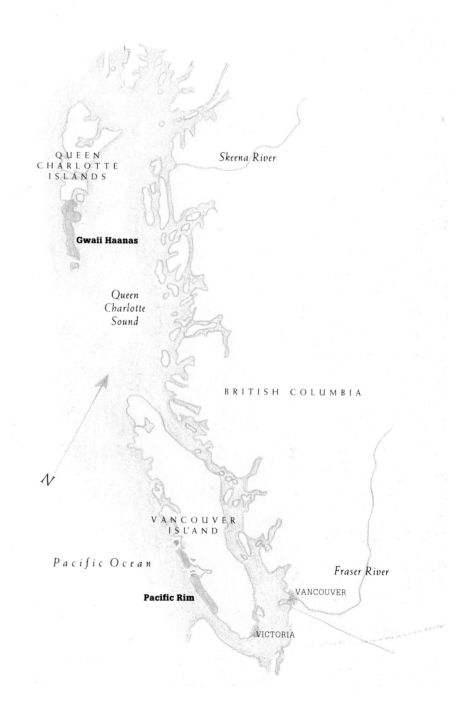

(65-foot) circumference, on Meares Island. So rich is the vegetation that the biomass (weight of plants per hectare) can reach levels of up to twice that of mature tropical rainforest.

Grizzly and black bears, cougar, and wolf are still found in this region's wilderness. Sperm whales, grey whales, killer whales, and blue whales still migrate through the Pacific waters and inland straits. Prime grizzly bear habitat is protected in the Khutzeymateen Valley grizzly bear reserve, and the Robson Bight Killer Whale Sanctuary protects sensitive killer whale rubbing beaches in Johnston Strait.

The Strait of Georgia Lowlands experience the warm, dry summers and mild winters characteristic of a Mediterranean climate. A diversity of vegetation, ranging from coastal Douglas fir to prickly pear cactus, as well as the extremely rare Garry oak, supports a range of species found nowhere else in Canada. The Fraser estuary contains areas critical for waterfowl and shorebirds, and is an annual stopover for millions of migrating birds.

The forestry, tourism, and fishing industries have prospered in this zone. The beauty and richness of the land continue to draw new residents and visitors from eastern Canada and other nations. And the once-plentiful trees and salmon support some of the most important industries. The continued exploitation of the ancient forests and increased urbanization in the Strait of Georgia region have, however, sparked a number of environmental campaigns. The Garry Oak Meadow Group, for example, is trying to save the last remnants of Garry oak–brome meadow ecosystems on eastern Vancouver Island, and a few of the Gulf Islands, and in the Fraser Valley.

Environmentalists are concerned over the rapid depletion of old-growth ecosystems and the resultant impact on plants, animals, and general environmental quality. The Sierra Club of Western Canada estimates that unless there is a significant reduction in the overall rate of logging on Vancouver Island, its temperate rainforest could well be liquidated by 2022.

Commercial pressures to log forests in such places as the Carmanah Valley, Clayoquot Sound, and Tsitika Valley, and to expand housing developments and forestry operations on the Gulf Islands, have made this natural zone one of Canada's most contentious environmental battlegrounds. Growing support for the protection of west coast wilderness areas, the expansion of a thriving eco-tourism sector, and a commitment by the British Columbia government to double the size of its provincial park and protected areas network are encouraging signs that additional wilderness areas will be preserved.

There have been some successes in protecting old-growth forests, as with the creation of the Gwaii Haanas National Park Reserve, the complete preservation of the Khutzeymateen Valley and the Megin River Valley in Clayoquot Sound. The old-growth forest of the Carmanah Valley, adjacent to Pacific Rim National Park Reserve on Vancouver Island, is now completely protected from logging.

The national parks in this zone, along with British Columbia's first provincial park, Strathcona, and other protected areas provide tremendous opportunities to kayak, hike, bike, sail, and camp. There are numerous areas providing a wide range of wildlife-viewing opportunities. Roosevelt elk graze in the woodlands at the north end of Strathcona Provincial Park. Boundary Bay is a critical stopover for migrating birds on the Pacific Flyway. Grey and humpback whales migrate along the coast of Pacific Rim National Park Reserve in spring and fall. And the black bears in Gwaii Haanas National Park Reserve are among the world's largest. Also on the Queen Charlotte Islands is the Delkatla Slough, a protected wildlife area on the north end of the island outside Masset.

Page 34: **A tide pool along the open Pacific coast is rimmed with mussels and filled with anemones and sea urchins.**

One hundred and thirty-eight islands and hundreds of islets are scattered within Gwaii Haanas National Park Reserve.

Spent surf runs across Long Beach, Pacific Rim National Park Reserve.

A lone sea star clings to a rock
in the intertidal zone of Pacific Rim
National Park Reserve.

The still waters of a tide pool provide a brief refuge for marine life from the incoming tide.

A full moon rises over Louscoone Point on the west

coast of Gwaii Haanas National Park Reserve.

Sea sacks bring some colour to the intertidal zone on the shore of Kunghit Island.

The totem poles on Sgan Gwaii (Anthony Island) are among the most evocative monuments created by the Haida people.

The old-growth wilderness on Moresby Island

rises above seaweed-covered rocks.

Travellers along the wild west side of Gwaii Haanas
are sometimes treated to the sight of spectacular
sunsets over the Pacific Ocean.

THE CANADIAN ROCKIES ARE ONE OF CANADA'S GREAT NATIONAL TREASURES. Their sweeping vistas, and the wildlife they support, have attracted tourists for decades. The jagged edges of the mountains, and the characteristic U-shaped valleys, are evidence of the powerful natural forces that have shaped them.

Ten years before the railway was pushed through the Western Mountains, this region was known mainly to native Indians and traders. A few intrepid explorers glimpsed the riches that were hidden there: David Thompson crossed Athabasca Pass in the winter of 1810–11; Sir George Simpson pioneered a new route across the central Rockies in 1841; and Major A.B. Rogers found the way through Rogers Pass in 1881 that became the route for the transcontinental railway. The railway, of course, was pivotal in opening up the mountains as well as the coast.

The Western Mountains zone comprises two of the national park system's natural regions: the Columbia Mountains to the west and the Rocky Mountains to the east. Seven national parks are located in this zone. The dominant feature, of course, is the mountains that trend northwest-southeast. The Western Mountains zone contains young mountains with many peaks, great local variations in elevation, extensive forests, and a teeming wildlife population. Glaciers and the rivers running off the ice packs have carved deep valleys and canyons throughout the region.

The Columbia Mountains feature narrow valleys squeezed between sheer mountain walls. Almost 23 metres (76 feet) of annual snowfall makes this avalanche and glacier country. The high moisture in the region has produced interior rainforests. Western red cedar and hemlock are found at low to middle elevations. Above that, and below the alpine tundra, are dense stands of Engelmann spruce, alpine fir, and lodgepole pine.

To the east, the Rocky Mountains straddle the Continental Divide of western North America. They form a series of parallel mountain ranges including the Western Ranges, the Main Ranges, the Front Ranges, and the Foothills. Visitors can observe the difference between these ranges by viewing the Foothills from Morley, Alberta, the Front Ranges from Banff townsite, the Main Ranges from Jasper townsite, and the Western Ranges from Radium. Together, the four mountain parks of Banff, Jasper, Kootenay, and Yoho contain a representative sample of each of the ranges and their characteristic vegetation and wildlife.

Tectonic forces squeezed and uplifted sediments to form the mountains. The Western Ranges are soft shales. The Main Ranges, underlain by quartzite and bordered by faults, were forced up as great rigid blocks. They contain the highest mountains in the four ranges. The Front Ranges are composed of limestone and shale and often have a tilted, tooth-like appearance. The Foothills, the eastern-most extension of the Rocky Mountains, are rounded, rolling hills that lie between the Front Ranges and the grasslands of Alberta.

Grizzly and black bear, mountain goats, bighorn sheep, mule deer and white-tailed deer, elk, moose, and wolves all thrive in this vertiginous habitat. A number of the species found in the Western Mountains need large territories to survive. Each grizzly bear in Alberta, for example, may need from 180 to 1,200 square kilometres (72 to 480 square miles). Thus, while the four mountain parks, along with a number of provincial parks and wilderness areas, form a large contiguous block of relatively undisturbed wilderness, land outside the parks must also be managed to support wildlife.

There are, in fact, wildlife viewing areas outside the national parks. The Columbia Wetlands, west of Kootenay National Park, is a good spot for viewing waterfowl, eagles, and the great horned owl. Black bear and moose can be seen in Wells Gray Provincial Park, where over 215 species of birds have been spotted. Grizzly bears gather on the banks of rivers during salmon runs in Bowron Lakes Provincial Park. A complete list of wildlife viewing areas can be found in the *British Columbia Wildlife Viewing Guide* by Bill Wareham.

There are two national parks representing the Columbia Mountains: Mount Revelstoke and Glacier. The four-mountain-park complex of Banff, Jasper, Kootenay, and Yoho, totalling almost 21,000 square kilometres (8,400 square miles) is one of the largest and best-known protected natural areas in the world. The parks were designated a UNESCO World Heritage Site in 1985. In addition, Waterton Lakes National Park in southwestern Alberta represents a unique portion of the Rocky Mountains, and is part of the international biosphere reserve network.

The transcontinental railway was completed in this region in 1885, but it was the Trans-Canada Highway, built in 1962, that gave millions of people access to the mountains. The result has been sustained heavy pressure on the fragile mountain ecology. A journey that took explorers weeks and months to complete in the nineteenth century can now be done in hours. Development of this zone for timber, oil, and gas continues to fragment the natural areas outside the national and provincial parks. Mountaineering, downhill skiing, backcountry hiking, and rafting are the dominant recreational activities. At work or play, we have made progress, perhaps, but progress itself has created new threats to the wilderness environment.

Page 46: **Pinnacle Mountain, viewed from Larch Valley in Banff National Park, is said to be the birthplace of recreational hiking in the Canadian Rockies.**

A carpet of wildflowers in an alpine meadow rewards visitors who make their way to the summit of Mount Revelstoke.

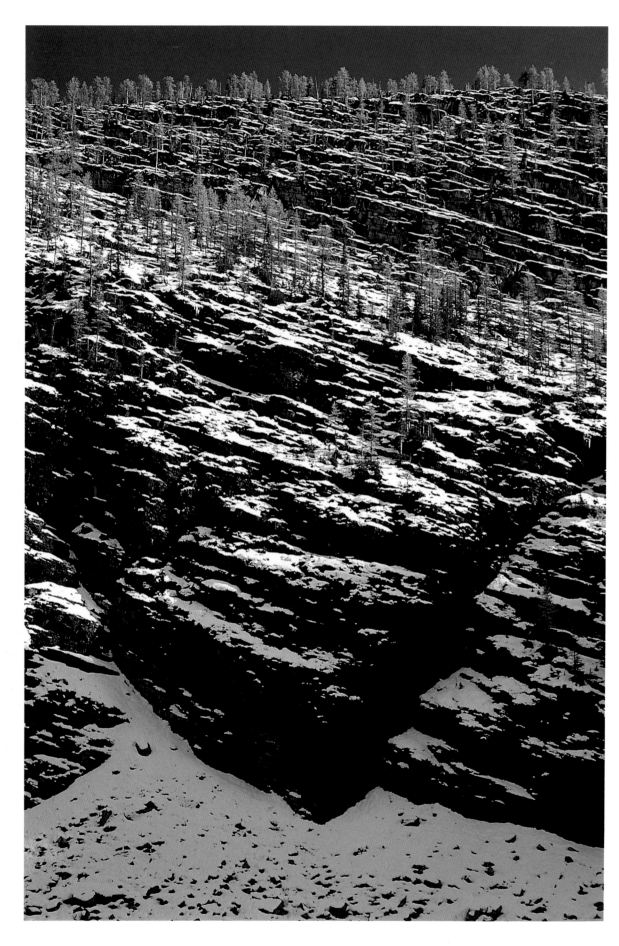

Alpine larch trees plastered with fresh snow display their autumn gold at the top of The Beehive, Banff National Park.

Wildflowers, such as the shrubby beard-tongue,

bring colour to the mountain landscape in Banff

National Park.

The glaciated east face of Mount Victoria towers
over canoeists on Lake Louise.

Tilted Mountain, part of the spectacular Slate Range,
rises above Baker Lake in the Skoki Valley region of
Banff National Park.

Snow covers a boulder field in Ermite Valley,
a region of spectacular alpine scenery, near the
Continental Divide in Jasper National Park.

A tall rock pinnacle stands guard over the north end of Lake McArthur in Yoho National Park.

Flowers contrast sharply with rock in Yoho National Park.

A break in the alpine larches reveals a glimpse of

Floe Lake in Kootenay National Park.

THE NORTHWESTERN MOUNTAINS

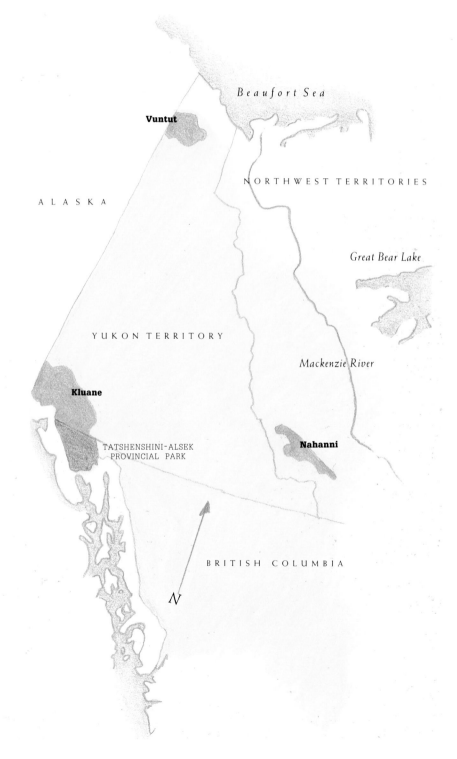

THIS IS A ZONE OF TREMENDOUS CONTRASTS. ALONG THE WEST COAST are some of the youngest landscapes in Canada, while some of the oldest, bypassed by the last advance of the glaciers, are in the northern Yukon. The land rises as one travels inland from the coastal forests of Sitka spruce, through river-carved canyons and over grasses, shrubs, and dwarf trees, to ice-covered Mount Logan, Canada's highest point at 5959 metres (19,548 feet). At the northern end of this zone is one of the world's most important wetlands, the Old Crow Flats. This is the Canadian wilderness at its finest and wildest.

Over 40,000 square kilometres (16,000 square miles) of this northern wilderness is protected in Kluane, Nahanni, Vuntut, and Ivvavik national parks. The June 1993 decision of the British Columbia government to create the Tatshenshini provincial wilderness park in the northwestern corner of the province, immediately south of Kluane National Park Reserve, is a most welcome and significant addition to the protected areas network in this region. Together with Alaska's Wrangell – St. Elias and Glacier Bay national parks, the Tatshenshini and Kluane parks form the largest internationally protected area in the world.

The Northern Coast Mountains, including Mount Logan, dominate the western portion of this zone. The characteristic features are the mountains themselves – the St. Elias Mountains and the Boundary Ranges – and the largest non-polar icefields in Canada. Glaciers hang off the mountains by the thousands. More than 2,000 glaciers are found just in Kluane National Park Reserve. Some of Canada's wildest rivers, the Tatshenshini-Alsek and the Stikine, cut across the landscape. The landforms studied in high school geography textbooks come alive: U-shaped and hanging valleys, cirques, moraines, and alluvial cones are all to be seen here

Mountains, plateaux, plains, and trenches characterize the Northern Interior Mountains and Plateaux region. It has been shaped by glaciers and volcanoes. Cinder cones and lava plains are found in the Mount Edziza Provincial Wilderness Park of British Columbia. Major rivers have carved deep canyons through this region, like the 100-metre (330-foot) Grand Canyon of the Stikine River. Conservation groups such as the Friends of the Stikine, the Valhalla Wilderness Society, and the Canadian Nature Federation have recommended that the federal government work with the British Columbia government to protect the Stikine watershed outside the Mount Edziza and Spatsizi provincial parks to protect the entire greater Stikine ecosystem.

If one natural feature has drawn popular attention to the Mackenzie Mountains, it is Virginia Falls on the South Nahanni River. The mountains and plateaux of this region are underlain by limestone, which has produced jagged mountains and deep canyons. In and around Nahanni National Park Reserve are some of the most spectacular karst formations in the world. Hotsprings, including the Rabbitkettle Hotsprings, the largest in Nahanni, are found in the mountains. The Government of the Northwest Territories has proposed the creation of a large territorial park to the north of Nahanni that would preserve some of the fascinating physical features that characterize this region.

The Northern Yukon natural region lies at the northernmost extremity of this zone. Here the continental mountains that form the backbone of western North America reach their most northerly extension. The eroded and rounded Richardson and British Mountains, the rolling Ogilvie Mountains, and the interior plains of the Old Crow Flats are the main characteristics of this region. The Firth River runs north through the northern Yukon, blanketed on both sides by alpine tundra. Part of the Old Crow Flats is protected in Vuntut National Park.

Habitats for some of the continent's most spectacular wildlife are either protected or still in a wild condition in this part of the world. In addition to the Porcupine caribou, there are grizzly bears, Dall sheep, wood caribou, mountain goat, wolf, and the rare trumpeter swan, whose breeding grounds are contained in this area.

The extensive wilderness that characterizes this area is always at risk to development. Proposed mining operations throughout the zone have threatened rivers such as the Tatshenshini and Nahanni. Unprotected rivers such as the Stikine remain at risk because of their vast hydroelectric power generating potential. A proposed pipeline across the coastal plain of the northern Yukon was finally prohibited when Ivvavik National Park was created in 1984.

Much of the area is subject to aboriginal land claims. Present and future generations of Canadians can enjoy Vuntut National Park – and Ivvavik to the north – because aboriginal peoples supported these parks and are willing to share the tremendous natural wonders of these landscapes with the rest of the nation.

Page 58: Mount Maxwell stands at the end of the Slims River Valley in Kluane National Park Reserve.

Dall sheep form a ragged line on the slopes
of the Hoge-Burwash Divide in Kluane National
Park Reserve.

Towers of ice, or "seracs," stand at the foot of
Donjek Glacier in Kluane National Park Reserve.

A hiker is dwarfed by a huge wall of ice as she walks

on the banks of the Donjek River.

The Donjek Glacier is one of many glaciers flowing

out of the St. Elias Mountains. Mount Logan,

Canada's highest mountain, is just visible on

the horizon.

The Ragged Range towers over Glacier Lake
northwest of Nahanni National Park Reserve — an
area Parks Canada hopes to add to the park at a
future date.

**The St. Elias Mountains in Kluane National Park
Reserve are the highest range of mountains in
North America.**

The north and south branches of the Kaskawulsh

Glacier join to form a wide river of ice in Kluane

National Park Reserve.

THE
INTERIOR
PLAINS

THE INTERIOR PLAINS ZONE STRETCHES FROM THE COASTAL PLAIN OF THE northern Yukon, through the northern boreal forests of Alberta and Saskatchewan, to the prairie grasslands of southern Canada. There are five natural regions in this geograhic zone: Mackenzie Delta, Northern Boreal Plains, Southern Boreal Plains and Plateaux, Prairie Grasslands, and Manitoba Lowlands. As its name suggests, the Interior Plains is relatively flat. Great herds of wildlife, such as caribou and bison, continue to roam throughout its northern section, but few of the pronghorn antelope, mule deer, and elk that once inhabited the southern section survive.

Some of Canada's more impressive water features are found here, including Canada's largest river, the Mackenzie, and its major tributaries such as the Liard, Peace, and Slave. Two major lakes dominate the north: Great Slave Lake and Great Bear Lake. The Peace–Athabasca Delta, one of the world's largest inland deltas, is an important migratory stopover for geese, swans, and ducks.

The land, its vegetation, and wildlife vary across the region. The Mackenzie Delta is a transition from flat, treeless tundra to stunted spruce forests, underlain by permafrost, and covered intermittently by flood water. This is the northern limit of the treeline. The highest concentration of pingos (cone-shaped hills with a core of ice) is found here, providing the only relief. Several are protected by the Pingos of Tuktoyaktuk Canadian Landmark, established under the 1984 Inuvialuit land-claim agreement with the government of Canada. Ivvavik National Park is found in this natural region. Immediately to the north, Ivvavik encloses the only non-glaciated mountain range in Canada, the British Mountains. Migrating through this portion of the park is the 180,000-strong Porcupine caribou herd, which the native people of Old Crow, Yukon, depend upon to support their traditional way of life.

The Northern Boreal Plains is a vast and wild plain of bogs, forests, and muskeg. The area is characterized by forests of open spruce to the north, and dense stands of spruce and tamarack to the south. Vast treeless tracts also dominate large parts of this region. Two bison herds are found here: wood bison in the Mackenzie Bison Sanctuary, and the world's largest free-roaming herd in Wood Buffalo National Park. Both herds are the product of conservation programs to stop the extinction of the plains and wood bison.

The Southern Boreal Plains and Plateaux region is a large transition zone, from the moist boreal forest to the north, to the dry and treeless prairies to the south. But it also features a transition from the relatively undeveloped wilderness areas of northern Canada to one of the most intensively altered landscapes in the south. There are three distinct vegetation zones: black spruce and muskeg; mixed forest containing balsam fir and black spruce; and aspen parkland. The aspen parkland is a globally unique natural community of trembling aspen and fescue prairie. Wood Buffalo, Elk Island, Prince Albert, and Riding Mountain national parks have representative features of this natural region.

The prairie grasslands, containing some of the richest soil and most productive growing conditions in Canada, have been reduced to a remnant ecosystem to support agriculture. Only 2 percent of this vast plain is left and, for this reason, many of Canada's endangered species are found here. A handful of native species can still be found, including pronghorn antelope, black-tailed prairie dogs, and burrowing owl. Some native prairie areas are protected within the relatively new Grasslands National Park, where a land-acquisition program is still underway. But even if Parks Canada is able to pur-

chase enough land so that the park achieves its maximum possible size of 900 square kilometres (360 square miles), it will not protect a self-sustaining ecosystem. A new national wildlife area has been established on the Canadian Forces Base Suffield near Wainwright, Alberta.

The only natural region within the Interior Plains not represented in the national park system is the Manitoba Lowlands. Located to the east of the Prairie Grasslands, the Manitoba Lowlands has a transition from white and black spruce in the north, to tall-grass prairie in the south. North America's largest freshwater delta remains relatively undisturbed at Delta Marsh. The federal government has identified a candidate national park to represent this natural region around the Limestone Bay and Long Point areas. Environmentalists are pressing for critical forests, caribou habitats, and karst caves to be added to the park.

The extent to which the southern portion of this natural zone has been developed is evident in the extensive grid pattern of roads and farms that covers its fertile soil. It is apparent around the existing national parks. Elk Island, Prince Albert, Riding Mountain, and Grasslands are all essentially ecological islands because of development on adjacent lands. A number of governments and conservation groups worked with World Wildlife Fund to produce the "Prairie Conservation Action Plan," a blueprint for protecting and restoring the biological diversity of the prairie. Action by the governments of Alberta, Saskatchewan, and Manitoba to complete their protected area networks is urgently needed to save a representative sample of each natural region within the Interior Plains zone.

Page 68: Clouds gather over Clear Lake, Riding Mountain National Park.

Lakes and ponds — more than 250 of them — make up 20 percent of Elk Island National Park.

Elk Island National Park protects an area of

increasingly rare aspen parkland.

A field of rush and other grasses tousled by northern winds in Wood Buffalo National Park.

Ivvavik National Park in the northern Yukon was the first national park in Canada to be established by a land-claim agreement between the federal government and Inuvialuit of the western Arctic.

Ivvavik protects only a part of the territory through which the Porcupine caribou herd migrates each year. The herd is still threatened by the possibility of oil development in Alaska.

THE
CANADIAN SHIELD

THE CANADIAN SHIELD COVERS MORE THAN 50 PERCENT OF THE COUNTRY, extending northward from the Great Lakes to the Arctic, and from the western Northwest Territories to the coast of Labrador. It is composed of material from the Precambrian span of geologic history, meaning that the rocks vary in age from three billion to six million years.

The first life including algae, fungi, and soft-bodied sea plants and animals evolved in Precambrian times. Some of the world's oldest mountains and mountain remnants are found in this zone. On exposed outcrops of the Canadian Shield one can find scratch marks and polished patches where glaciers scraped the rock during their last advance and retreat, some 10,000 to 15,000 years ago.

There are fourteen national park natural regions within the Canadian Shield zone, including two that are more characteristic of the Hudson Bay Lowlands located at the southern end of Hudson Bay. Only five of the fourteen natural regions are represented in the seven national parks located here. And two of them are among the smallest national parks in Canada. The seven parks are Tuktut Nogait, Auyuittuq, Wapusk, Pukaskwa, La Mauricie, Georgian Bay Islands, and the St. Lawrence Islands.

To briefly describe fourteen natural regions is difficult. However, there are three basic sub-zones here: the taiga shield, the boreal shield, and the Hudson Plains. The taiga shield is located on the east and west side of Hudson Bay and is the northernmost sub-zone. This area is typified by Precambrian bedrock outcrops, rolling plains, and hundreds of lakes. To the northwest, eskers and drumlins are found amid a polar tundra desert. The limits of tree growth are seen here, where forests are open lichen woodlands that turn into open arctic tundra as you head north.

Potential national parks in this sub-zone include Wager Bay in the Northwest Territories, Lac Guillaume Delisle in Quebec, and the Torngat Mountains in Labrador. In 1970 over 7,100 square kilometres (2,840 square miles) of land were withdrawn from development for the proposed East Arm of Great Slave Lake national park. No progress has been made because of lack of support from a local native community

Some of the last pristine wilderness areas are found and protected in the taiga shield zone. Canada's two largest protected areas, the Queen Maude Gulf Migratory Bird Sanctuary at 62,000 square kilometres (24,800 square miles), and the Thelon Game Sanctuary, 55,000 square kilometres (22,000 square miles), are found here. Grizzly bears, muskoxen, white wolves, and polar bears all roam the primeval wilderness. The last nesting grounds of the Eskimo curlew, one of the rarest birds in Canada, are also here.

The boreal shield is a U-shaped sub-zone extending east from northern Saskatchewan, below Hudson Bay, through to the Labrador coast. It contains the southern boundary of the Canadian Shield, located above the Great Lakes and St. Lawrence River. Coniferous trees and spruce forests dominate the northern section, with deciduous, broad-leaf trees such as sugar maple and American bass to the south. Wildlife found in this area includes woodland caribou, black bear, bobcat, boreal owl, and evening grosbeak. Two potential new national parks in this region include the Mealy Mountains in southern Labrador, and the Hautes Gorges region near Charlevoix, Quebec.

Provincial governments have created a number of wilderness parks in this sub-zone. Ontario created Woodland Caribou wilderness park in 1983, immediately adjacent to Manitoba's Atikaki Provincial Park. The Saskatchewan government established the Athabasca Sand Dunes wilderness park in 1992. And the Quebec government withdrew 3.5 million hectares (9 million acres) of wilderness from development in order to plan precise boundaries for twenty new provincial parks that should be approved in the near future.

The largest extent of wetlands in Canada is found within the Hudson Bay plains sub-zone, which extends around the southern portions of Hudson and James bays from Manitoba to Quebec. Muskeg and marshes dominate the landscape where elevations seldom exceed 500 metres (1,640 feet) above sea level. This sub-zone is relatively treeless because of the predominance of wetlands and soil that is nutrient-deficient and highly acidic. Beluga and bowhead whales find an important summer habitat in the saltwater bays that are found here. Ontario's largest provincial park, Polar Bear, is located here. And the governments of Canada and Manitoba concluded an agreement in 1996 creating Wapusk National Park, near Churchill.

A number of developments continue to erode the Shield wilderness. Forests in the south continue to be allocated to development and to be exploited. The large hydroelectric developments at Baie James I, and proposed for the Whale River, are located on the eastern shores of Hudson Bay. Given the paucity of wilderness areas preserved from a growing number of industrial developments in this zone, a greater portion of the Canadian Shield must be safeguarded within national parks and other protected areas by the turn of the century.

Page 76: Le Passage, at the northern end of Lake Wapizagonke in La Mauricie National Park, has seen the coming and going of glaciers, wildlife, nomadic hunters, lumberjacks, and most recently, canoeists.

Broad-leafed willow herb grows on the sandy floor
of Weasel Valley, the major hiking route through
Auyuittuq National Park Reserve.

Auyuittuq, Baffin Island. In Inuit, the park's name

means "the place that does not melt."

Autumn leaves, Beausoleil Island, Georgian Bay Islands National Park.

After the leaves have fallen, and as winter draws closer, the number of park visitors declines, providing nature with a respite from the wear and tear of heavy recreational use.

The spectacular autumn colours draw many
visitors to La Mauricie National Park each year.

The Lake Superior shore off Pukaskwa National
Park can be as wild and desolate as any Canadian
wilderness region.

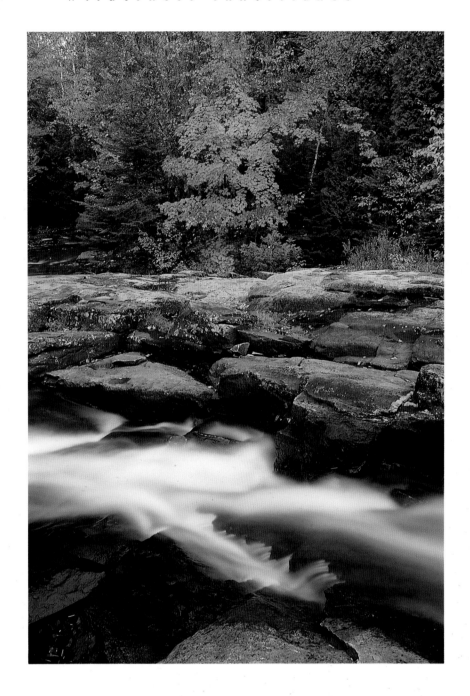

La Mauricie, Quebec's second national
park, encloses representative examples of the
mountains, forests, lakes, and rivers of the
Quebec Laurentians.

A boulder of Precambrian rock, veined with
quartzite, lies on the wild coast of Lake Superior
near Fisherman River, Pukaskwa National Park.

Yellow shrubby cinquefoil and white ox-eye
daisies are nestled among rocks in Pukaskwa
National Park.

THE ST. LAWRENCE LOWLANDS

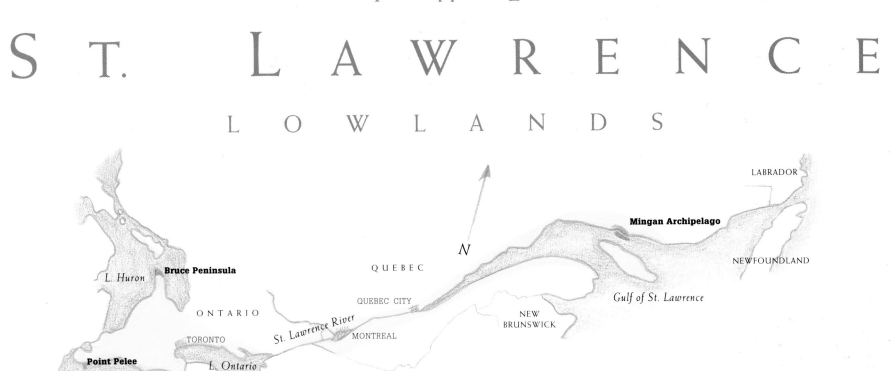

TUCKED UNDER THE SOUTHERN EXTREMITY OF THE CANADIAN SHIELD, THE St. Lawrence Lowlands zone contains the greatest number of plants and animals found in Canada. This region is made up of three separate sub-regions that extend from the Gulf of St. Lawrence to Manitoulin Island and Lake Huron. Two national parks are located in the western sub-region, only one in the eastern sub-region, and none in the central sub-region.

The westerly sub-region is a triangle that extends from Georgian Bay to the eastern limit of Lake Ontario, and includes all of southwestern Ontario down to Point Pelee. Cutting through this zone is the Niagara Escarpment, which extends from Niagara Falls to Hamilton, and on up to the Bruce Peninsula. The Carolinian forest zone, located in the southern part of the subregion, contains some of the most diverse, and threatened, flora and fauna in Canada. Half the Canadian human population lives in this and the central sub-regions. Reptiles including the eastern tiny soft-shelled turtle, Massasauga rattler, and eastern Canada's only lizard, the five-lined skink, are found here, but with increasing rarity.

The eastern zone is located in the Gulf of St. Lawrence and includes Anticosti Island and the Mingan Archipelago on the north shore of Quebec. The archipelago is protected within the Mingan Archipelago National Park Reserve, which the federal government purchased from Dome Petroleum in 1983. Puffins and other seabirds, along with whales and seals, feed in the offshore waters. The tidal flats of the Cap Tourmente National Wildlife Area are host to thousands of snow geese during their migration. The vegetation in this zone is characterized by boreal species such as white and black spruce and, in the damp habitats, balsam fir.

Three small national parks are located in this zone, while a fourth, Georgian Bay Islands, straddles both the St. Lawrence Lowlands and the Canadian Shield. The Bruce Peninsula National Park protects the spectacular northern tip of the Niagara Escarpment. It, along with Mingan Archipelago park and Canada's first national marine park, Fathom Five, protects rock pillars or stacks, such as Flowerpot Island. The national marine park system is designed to represent each of the four Great Lakes fully in Canada, plus Georgian Bay. Point Pelee is one of Canada's most popular bird-watching areas and contains the southernmost point on the Canadian mainland.

It will be no easy matter to establish a national park within the central sub-region. This region was among the first settled by Europeans, and has been intensively developed for urban and agricultural use for more than 300 years. The Mount St. Hilaire biosphere reserve, south of Montreal, protects a natural area on this Monteregion hill. Mount Royal Park, while hardly a wilderness park, is a major urban park protecting a large natural area in the centre of Montreal. Frederick Law Olmsted, the renowned American landscape architect who designed Central Park in New York and produced the first plan for Yosemite National Park, also designed Mount Royal.

The ecological significance of the area has been given international recognition. Mount St. Hilaire, the Niagara Escarpment, and Long Point are unesco biosphere reserves because they contain protected natural features within highly developed areas. And the wetland areas conserved within Point Pelee National Park as well as three national wildlife areas – Long Point, Lac St. Francois, and St. Clair – are all designated as Ramsar sites, meaning they are designated as wetlands of international significance under a UNESCO convention signed in 1971 in Ramsar, Iran.

In December 1997, Parliament passed legislation that finally created the Saguenay–St. Lawrence Estuary marine region. Located at the confluence of the Saguenay River and the St. Lawrence Estuary northeast of Quebec City, it is an important conservation tool in the fight to save the endangered beluga whale. This new park is home to the only southern beluga population, and will be jointly managed by the federal and Quebec governments.

Stronger conservation practices are required throughout this natural region if these parks are to maintain their integrity and if the multiplicity of plant and animal life that characterizes this zone is to survive.

Page 88: **The view from the tip of Point Pelee National Park, the most southerly point on the Canadian mainland.**

Silverweed finds a tenuous home in the rock of the Mingan Archipelago.

A natural limestone sculpture looms over a visitor to

Mingan Archipelago National Park Reserve.

The white birch trees and pale cobblestones on the
Georgian Bay coast of Bruce Peninsula National
Park stand in stark contrast to the dark limestone
cliffs that characterize this landscape.

Erosion by wind and sea has given each rugged
island in the Mingan Archipelago National Park
Reserve a unique, sculpted appearance.

The harsh conditions and limestone terrain that predominate in the Mingan Islands support only a tundra-like vegetation.

THE
APPALACHIANS

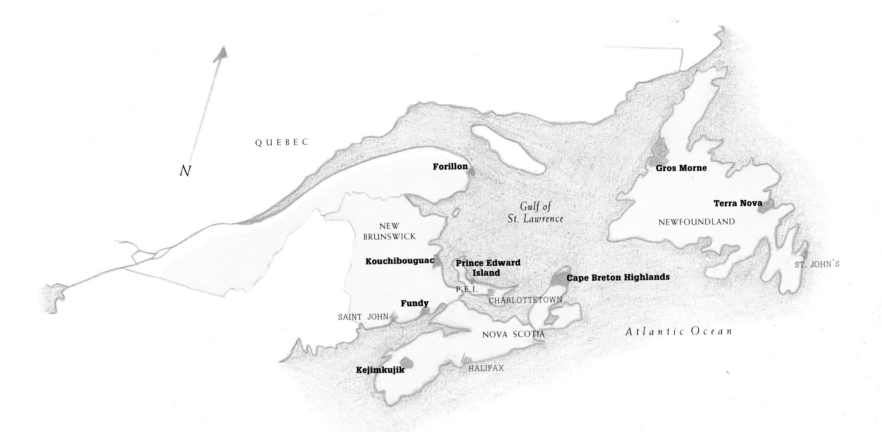

MOST CANADIANS KNOW THIS ZONE AS ATLANTIC CANADA, OR THE MARITIMES. It includes the four maritime provinces along with the Gaspésie peninsula. It is here that the Appalachian Mountains reach their northern extremity. And while the Appalachians contain the most spectacular mountain scenery east of the Rockies, it is the ocean that dominates and nurtures much of the life in this part of Canada.

Centuries of human occupation and development have altered much of this zone. Logging and agriculture have removed many of the original forests, including some of those within national parks such as Fundy and Kouchibouguac. Hunting and habitat loss have contributed to the extirpation of the wolf and caribou in a number of areas, such as the Maritime Plain natural region. Depletion of the cod fishery has produced an ecological and economic crisis in the outport communities of Newfoundland.

Eight national parks are located in this zone, which contains six of the national park natural regions. Each and every national park borders on the ocean, including Kejimkujik, which has a 22-square-kilometre (9-square-mile) adjunct at Port Mouton, one of the least disturbed shoreline areas on the south coast of Nova Scotia. The federal government considers all six natural regions to be fully represented within the national park system. Because of their proximity to the ocean and extensive tourism infrastructure, these are among the most popular national parks.

The Shickshock Mountains of Quebec rise to flat-topped summits of over 900 metres (3,000 feet) in the eastern portion of this zone. Mount Jacques Cartier is the tallest at 1,320 metres (4,330 feet). Driving inland from the St. Lawrence River side of the Gaspé Peninsula, the visitor is suddenly confronted with quickly rising mountain walls. Several arctic and alpine species of wildlife, normally seen in the Arctic or Rockies, are found on the exposed summits and cliffs of these mountains. Development has reduced a once-flourishing caribou herd to a single remnant population in Gaspésie Provincial Park. Forillon National Park, at the tip of the Gaspé Peninsula, represents the Notre Dame Mountains natural region along with the boreal forest and coastal features of this zone.

To the east is the Maritime Acadian Highlands, a rolling plateau averaging 300 metres (980 feet) above sea level that includes a wide swath of land around the Bay of Fundy, and Cape Breton Island. A region of contrasts, the Bay of Fundy includes cliffs of sedimentary rock, mud flats, and salt marshes. Some of the world's highest tides are found here. The forests on the New Brunswick side of Fundy are dominated by red spruce, while white spruce characterizes the Nova Scotia side. Fundy National Park in New Brunswick includes representative features of the Fundy coast and the Caledonia Highlands. The upland plateaux of Cape Breton Island are barrenlands where Labrador tea, a boreal shrub, is common. The scenic Cabot Trail winds through the spectacular and rugged coastal scenery of this region.

To the north of the Maritime Acadian Highlands is the Maritime Plain natural region of the national park system. Here are two very popular national parks – Prince Edward Island and Kouchibouguac. The extensive beaches, sand dunes, salt marshes, and warm lagoons found in these two parks are characteristic of this natural region. Offshore are the sparsely vegetated and constantly shifting barrier islands and reefs that protect the shoreline from storms moving through the Gulf of St. Lawrence. The beaches and sand dunes provide a critical nesting habitat for the endangered piping plover. Wolf, caribou, and marten have disappeared because much of this region has been logged or farmed.

The province of Newfoundland has two distinct natural regions. Gros Morne National Park represents the Western Newfoundland Highlands. The spectacular fiord of Western Brook Pond, one of Newfoundland's most photographed natural features, is characteristic of the Long Range Mountains that rise above the waters and beaches off the west coast. Beware the tangled Tuckamore stands of spruce and fir that grow on the exposed ridges of the Long Range Mountains. Caribou are found in this region, feeding off the lichens and caribou moss. The vegetation in the northwestern part of Newfoundland changes from boreal forest to forest-tundra. Here is L'Anse aux Meadows, site of the oldest known European settlement in the New World.

The Eastern Newfoundland Atlantic natural region and Terra Nova National Park are the most easterly natural region and national park in Canada. Here are the eroded remains of the Appalachian Mountains, inland lakes, and fast-flowing rivers. Almost half the region supports boreal forests of black spruce and balsam fir with bogs interspersed among them. Some of North America's largest seabird rookeries are found on the east coast of Newfoundland: Cape St. Mary's and Witless Bay are among the most spectacular in the world. Kittiwakes, puffins, common murres, and razor-billed auks number in the hundreds of thousands. The caribou in this region are the largest in North America.

The Newfoundland government established the largest protected wilderness area in the Maritimes in 1990 when it created the Bay du Nord Wilderness Reserve, which is over 3,450 square kilometres (1,380 square miles) in size. The Avalon Wilderness Reserve protects caribou and their habitat in the centre of the Avalon Peninsula. Each of the maritime provinces has at least one wetland habitat designated as a Ramsar site in recognition of its international conservation value.

Page 96: The Atlantic Ocean pounds the east coast of Cape Breton Highlands National Park

Ferns, Kejimkujik National Park.

Fresh water flows into the Bay of Fundy at Herring Cove, Fundy National Park.

Sand and sea meet in constantly changing combinations in Prince Edward Island National Park.

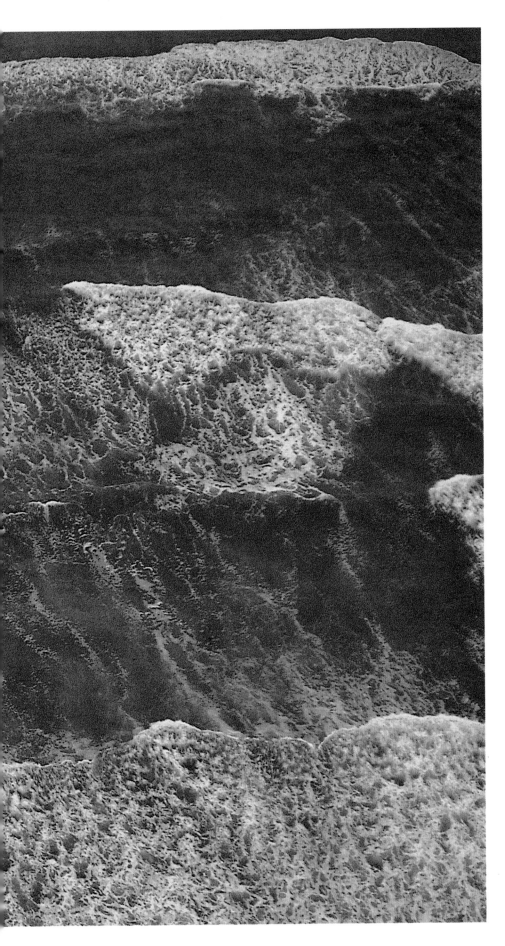

An aerial view of waves breaking on a beach in Prince Edward Island National Park.

The Mackenzie River makes its winding way to the sea at the northern end of Cape Breton Island.

The St. Catherines River Beach in the Seaside Adjunct of Kejimkujik National Park is an important breeding habitat for the endangered piping plover.

A gull appears to be unperturbed by the violence
of the surf breaking a few feet away at the tip of
Middle Head Peninsula, Cape Breton Highlands
National Park.

Picturesque Mary Ann Falls, Cape Breton Highlands National Park.

THE
ARCTIC LOWLANDS
AND ISLANDS

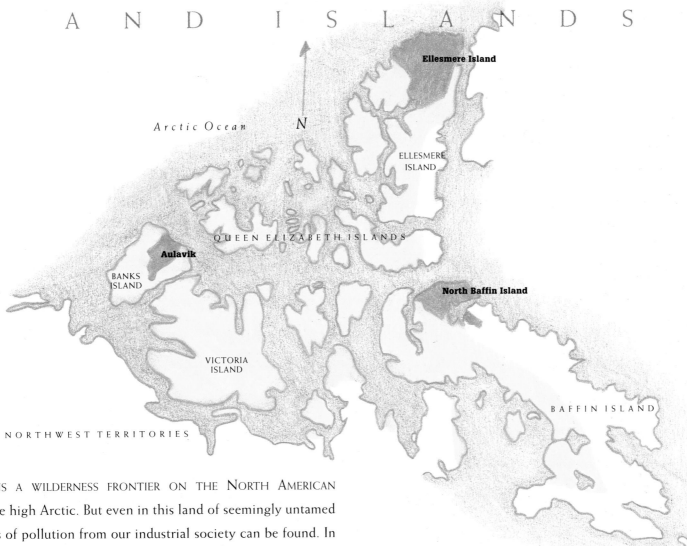

Ellesmere Island

Arctic Ocean

N

ELLESMERE
ISLAND

QUEEN ELIZABETH ISLANDS

Aulavik

North Baffin Island

BANKS
ISLAND

VICTORIA
ISLAND

BAFFIN ISLAND

NORTHWEST TERRITORIES

IF THERE REMAINS A WILDERNESS FRONTIER ON THE NORTH AMERICAN continent, it is the high Arctic. But even in this land of seemingly untamed wilderness, traces of pollution from our industrial society can be found. In spring, chemicals are carried over the Arctic that, under particular weather conditions, eat away at the ozone layer of Earth's atmosphere. Scientists are working to assess the impact of ozone depletion on arctic ecosystems. It is certain, however, that it is a stress this fragile natural world can do without.

The Arctic is not one vast, barren landscape. The national park system recognizes four distinct natural regions within it. Two are represented by large national parks: Aulavik National Park on Banks Island, and Ellesmere Island National Park Reserve on northern Ellesmere Island. The government of Canada and the Inuit of the eastern Arctic are committed to establishing a new national park on northern Baffin Island to represent a third

natural region. In 1992 the federal government legally withdrew the lands for the park from development, and it will become an official national park once Canada and the Inuit agree on the terms of its joint management.

The Western Arctic Lowlands natural region includes the western portion of the Northwest Passage and Victoria Island, which is larger than the four maritime provinces combined. Most of the land is sparsely vegetated. There is, however, a heavy cover of sedges, cotton grass, and mosses in wet areas. Only muskoxen and caribou remain in this area during the winter while most of the bird life migrates south. The twenty-four-hour sunshine of the summer brings life to this region as flocks of snow geese and other water-fowl return.

The Eastern Arctic Lowlands include the eastern portion of the North-west Passage and the internationally significant Lancaster Sound, which supports a variety of wildlife. Summer is short. The climate is cold, and overcast conditions prevail most of the time. There is some diversity in the landscape: 10-kilometre (6-mile)-wide tidal flats are found on the coast. Flat, marshy plains mixed with exposed rocks and lakes are found inland. And, to the north, the land rises to high plateaux, with spectacular fiords cutting inland beneath 1,000-metre (3,280-foot) cliffs. Polar bears cruise the coast for winter denning and spring seal hunting. Caribou, wolf, arctic fox, and arctic hare are plentiful in some of the more productive areas of this region.

The Western High Arctic is a polar desert, described by Parks Canada as "a frigid, barren rock-strewn land." Nowhere in this arid archipelago can you stand more than 50 kilometres (30 miles) from the sea. Little more than 10 centimetres (4 inches) of precipitation falls a year making this one of the driest landscapes on the planet. Snow may fall in any month. There is little or no vegetation. Polar bears, Peary caribou, muskox, arctic wolf, and arctic fox are concentrated around the wet lowlands. There is no national park in this region, but critical wetland nesting habitats for birds, calving habitats for muskox, and a polar bear route are protected in Polar Bear Pass National Wildlife Area.

The most northerly natural region in the national park system is called the Eastern High Arctic Glacier. This is as far away as you can get in Canada.

According to Parks Canada: "Here is a land of desolation and splendour on a grand scale. But it is also a land of intimate, fragile beauty – of delicate arctic poppies vibrating in the breeze, of miniature forests of lichens and heather, of subtle pastel shades and heady aromas." Several arctic thermal oases are to be found in Ellesmere Island National Park Reserve. In these oases, such as Lake Hazen, conditions support a variety of lush plants, including heather, blueberries, sedges, and mosses.

According to arctic researcher Edmund Carpenter, quoted by Barry Lopez in his book *Arctic Dreams*, "The landscape conveys an impression of absolute permanence. It is not hostile. It is simply there – untouched, silent, and complete. It is very lonely, yet the absence of all human traces gives you the feeling you understand this land and can take your place in it." Perhaps some of the new northern national parks will make it possible for more Canadians to experience wilderness in its true form.

In his report of the Mackenzie Valley Pipeline Inquiry, Thomas Berger urged Canadians to preserve the wilderness character of northern Canada: "If we are to preserve wilderness areas in the North, we must do so now. The available areas will diminish with each new industrial development on the frontier." Shortly after Berger filed his report in 1977, Parks Canada announced plans to create five new national wilderness parks in the north. To date, three of these national parks have been established. One was dropped because of mineral conflicts, while negotiations continue on the fifth, Wager Bay, on the northern coast of Hudson Bay.

Page 108: **Despite its harsh climate, Ellesmere Island's animal and plant life is rich and diverse.**

Snow and ice in Ellesmere Island National Park Reserve.

A pocket of broad-leafed willow herb marks the
return of the brief but intense growing season
on Baffin Island.

Ellesmere Island National Park Reserve, Canada's
second-largest national park, is among the most
remote and least accessible.

There are few locations more remote than the roadless wilderness of Ellesmere Island National Park Reserve.

Ice and mountains are the features that define our vision of the remote northern wilderness, Ellesmere Island National Park Reserve.

Sculpted icebergs slide majestically in front of the
rugged Grant Land Mountains, Ellesmere Island
National Park Reserve.

Land has been set aside for a national

park on northern Baffin Island.

THE PARKS

"The more parks are used, the more difficult it is to prevent abuse. . . .

The parks may lose the very thing that distinguished them from the outside world."

JAMES BERNARD HARKIN, COMMISSIONER, PARKS BRANCH, 1911 TO 1936

Page 118: **The cliffs of Cap-Bon-Ami and Cap-Gaspé are just visible at dusk from the Des-Rosiers campground, Forillon National Park.**

The Thomsen River flows lazily through the tundra landscape of Aulavik National Park on Banks Island.

AULAVIK

Almost twice the size of Prince Edward Island, Aulavik National Park protects the world's richest muskox habitat and a large portion of the Thomsen River watershed. One of Canada's newest national parks, Aulavik is located at the northern end of Banks Island, Northwest Territories, about 250 kilometres (155 miles) northeast of Sachs Harbour, the only community on the island. Negotiations for the new park were successfully concluded in August 1992, almost fourteen years after it was first proposed by the federal government as part of its "6 North of 60°," a program that sought to establish five new national parks and one Canadian landmark in northern Canada.

Aulavik, which means "place where people travel," was chosen by a native elder in Sachs Harbour as the name for the park. The park represents the ecological features of the Western Arctic Lowlands region of the national park system. Banks Island is characterized by rolling hills, meandering rivers and streams, and spectacular sea cliffs. Almost 40,000 muskoxen are on Banks Island, one of the highest concentrations of muskoxen in the world.

The Thomsen River basin is the core of the park, providing important lowland habitats for the large muskoxen population, and constituting the major route for visitors to the park. Only a few patches of fast water break the Thomsen's gentle flow over an extensive sand and gravel bed, and between watery meadows, oxbow lakes, and stretches of tundra ponds, on its way to McClure Strait. There are no white-water rapids, making this a canoeable river for people with minimal paddling experience. Wilderness survival skills, however, are critical given this park's isolation. In the brief, yet intense,

summer, green sedge meadows, dotted with white tufts of cotton grass and colourful arctic flowers, carpet the Thomsen River valley.

The Thomsen's major tributaries, such as the Musk Ox River and Able Creek, flow through deeply cut canyons and desert-like badlands. These areas, along with rugged seacoasts, barren rocky uplands, and polar deserts, provide a stunning contrast to the peaceful Thomsen and its surrounding meadows. Flanking the Thomsen River valley are a rugged plateau to the east, and an upland to the west, marked by ravines and valleys. Gyrfalcon Bluff rises from the eastern plateau, providing a 100-metre (328-foot)-high vantage point overlooking Mercy Bay. Fossilized plant stems and ferns are embedded in the valleys of the western uplands.

Mercy Bay is where the H.M.S. *Investigator*, commanded by Captain Robert M'Clure, was eventually abandoned in 1853 because it was ice-bound. The "copper Eskimos" of Victoria Island learned about the ship and, travelling the Thomsen, recovered iron, canvas, wood, copper sheathing, wool, and other material. Over 150 campsites where they killed muskoxen for food remain visible.

The diverse wildlife community in Aulavik National Park is protected as much as it can be from the harsh elements in this arctic wilderness. The

---

Aulavik National Park

- Territory: Northwest Territories
- Agreement in principle: 1992
- Size: 12,200 square kilometres (4,710 square miles)
- Local Community: Sachs Harbour

- Access: By air charter only
- Contact: Superintendent, Western Arctic District, Parks Canada, Box 1840, Inuvik, Northwest Territories X0E 0T0; telephone (403) 979-3248

muskoxen herd on Banks Island, of which 10,000 are found in the Thomsen River valley, has made a spectacular comeback from the brink of extinction at the beginning of the century. The muskox is one of several large species of wildlife to have survived North America's ice ages. Almost 25,000 lesser snow geese and up to 5,000 brants use the watery maze of streams, lakes, and ponds along the Thomsen River for moulting and staging in the summer months, although yearly numbers vary greatly. A subspecies of caribou unique to Banks Island has been produced from interbreeding between barren-ground and Peary caribou.

Banks Island has been used by the Inuvialuit and their ancestors as hunting territory for more than 3,400 years, and the park agreement signed by the Government of Canada and the Inuvialuit creating Aulavik National Park guarantees the continuation of their traditional resource-harvesting activities. In *Arctic Dreams*, author Barry Lopez reports that the Inuit do not hunt or trap on the northeastern part of Banks Island in the Thomsen River area, regarding it as an oasis that produces wildlife for human use. Remains from ancient Inuit cultures suggest that their way of life was based on muskox hunting and bowhead whaling. Hunting trips to Banks Island became more frequent after 1920 when the island was declared a game reserve for Inuit use only. Sachs Harbour became the first settlement on Banks Island in the early 1950s. The Inuvialuit will obtain employment benefits and business opportunities from the park and the tourist activity it will generate.

The new park provides the visitor with a unique arctic wilderness experience – travelling the most northerly navigable river in Canada by canoe or raft. There are innumerable opportunities to observe and photograph muskoxen and other arctic wildlife, and to view archaeological features that provide a deeper understanding and appreciation of the peoples of northern Canada and their culture.

AUYUITTUQ

Auyuittuq National Park Reserve is located almost entirely within the Arctic Circle, on the north shore of Baffin Island's Cumberland Peninsula. The twenty-four hours of daylight in the summer tempt visitors to revel in the spectacular scenery of this arctic wilderness for as long as they can stay awake. Auyuittuq – the word means "the land that never melts" – is a rugged mountain tundra park dominated by the Penny Ice Cap, which covers one-third of the park area; active glaciers and deep valleys and fiords. The peaks of Odin and Thor tower over the scenery in this land of giants; Thor, at 1,500 metres (4,920 feet), may be one of the tallest cliffs in the world.

The Eastern Baffin Island Shelf marine region and the Northern Davis natural region of the national park system are represented in Auyuittuq National Park Reserve. The federal government's plans to establish this national park, along with Kluane and Nahanni, were announced in 1972 by the Hon. Jean Chrétien, and all three parks became protected under the *National Parks Act* in 1974, fulfilling the government's commitment to preserve in perpetuity some of the grandeur and wilderness that is Canada's north.

Auyuittuq was designated a national park reserve when it was first protected under the *National Parks Act*, pending the resolution of land-claim negotiations between the Inuit and the government of Canada. A comprehensive land-claim agreement was reached in 1993. Auyuittuq National Park Reserve will be formally designated a national park once the government and the Inuit have concluded an agreement that will more fully define the economic benefits of the park to the Inuit.

The stupendous cliffs of Mount Breidablik and the
overhanging face of Mount Thor in the distance
dominate Auyuittuq National Park Reserve.

A park warden at work in Auyuittuq
National Park Reserve.

A deep and narrow mountain pass called Aksayook Pass, formerly known as Pangnirtung Pass, is a valley encircled by mountains, connecting North and South Pangnirtung Fjord. The highest point in Aksayook Pass is 400 metres (1,312 feet). The pass is the backbone of the one major trail used by hikers. Some of the trail is marked by stone cairns shaped like human figures – Inuksuit (singular is Inukshuk), which is Inuktitut for "looks like a person." By travelling the entire length of the pass – 97 kilometres (60 miles) – you end up crossing the Cumberland Peninsula.

While glaciers as long as 25 kilometres (15 miles) hang from the mountains, some of which are 2,000 metres (6,560 feet) high, the valley used by hikers is ice-free during the short summer months. Vegetation is sparse in certain areas, but lichens, mosses, sedges, and flowering plants such as the arctic poppy predominate in the valleys, giving the area some colour. While few birds winter over, about forty bird species represent most of Auyuittuq's wildlife. Besides the fifteen species of waterfowl such as loons, eider ducks, and murres, hikers can see ptarmigan, glaucous gull, and snowy owl. Peregrine

falcons and gyrfalcons nest in the crevices of rock walls or on the edge of cliffs. Mammals commonly found in the park include lemmings and arctic hare and fox. Polar bears inhabit the coast with other marine mammals. Caribou and wolf can be found inland.

Three interpretive themes reveal the natural and human history of Auyuittuq National Park Reserve: "Arctic Wilderness"; "History of the Eastern Arctic and the Inuit Cultural Tradition"; and "Origins of the Landscape: Glacial and Geomorphological History." Like many of Canada's national parks, Auyuittuq offers a unique opportunity to learn about the culture of Canada's first peoples.

One of the challenges in managing Auyuittuq is to disperse visitor use and to monitor the status of archaeological sites. This northern wilderness can be adversely affected by a stream of tourists travelling the same route year after year. Since Parks Canada is concerned about this issue, it may be wise to inquire about other places to see in and around Auyuittuq National Park Reserve when planning a visit.

BANFF

If there is one name that is synonymous with national parks in Canada, it is Banff, the birthplace of Canada's national park system. Banff (then called Rocky Mountain Park) was first established as a 26-square-kilometre (10-square-mile) reserve to protect the mineral hot springs on Sulphur Mountain from private development and settlement. The *Rocky Mountain Park Act* of 1887 expanded the reserve to 673 square kilometres (260 square miles) and formally established it as a park. The Lake Louise area was set aside in 1892

Auyuittuq National Park Reserve

- **Territory: Northwest Territories/Nunavut**
- **Date Established: 1976**
- **Size: 21,470 square kilometres (8,588 square miles)**
- **Visits: About 400 per year**
- **Campsites: Three designated back country, plus random camping**
- **Trails: Aksayook Pass is the one main trail route**

- **Access: By private outfitters' boat, snowmobile, hiking, cross-country skiing**
- **Local Communities: Pangnirtung and Broughton Island by scheduled air service**
- **Contact: Superintendent, Auyuittuq National Park Reserve, Box 353, Pangnirtung, Northwest Territories X0A 0R0; telephone (819) 473-8828**

Every year more hikers are dazzled by autumn's splendour in the alpine larch forests of Banff National Park.

to preserve its spectacular scenery, and was added to Rocky Mountain Park in 1902. After a number of boundary changes, Banff National Park is now slightly larger than Prince Edward Island.

Rocky Mountain Park was renamed Banff National Park in 1930. The name Banff was first used in 1883–84 for a Canadian Pacific Railway station located east of the hot springs. It was chosen by Lord Strathcona and other prominent individuals with the Canadian Pacific Railway and the Hudson's Bay Company. It was named after the town of Banff in the county of Banffshire near Lord Strathcona's birthplace in eastern Scotland. Banff is derived from "Bunnaimb," Gaelic for "mouth of the river."

Banff National Park, together with Jasper, Kootenay, Yoho, and

In 1887, the town of Banff included six hotels and nine shops. One hundred and eighty townsite lots had been leased to settlers.

Waterton Lakes national parks, represents the natural features of the Rocky Mountains, specifically the Main and Front ranges of the larger continental ranges system, within natural region 5 of the national park system. The Main and Front ranges constitute the two major mountain ranges in Banff. Mount Rundle is characteristic of the former, and Temple Mountain of the latter. The park contains at least twenty-five mountain peaks over 3,000 metres (9,842 feet) in height. The mountains tower over the alpine valleys, lakes, mountain rivers, and glaciers that characterize this park.

There are three major life zones in this park – the alpine, subalpine, and montane zones – and visitors are encouraged to experience them. The alpine region is devoid of trees because of its harsh climate at higher elevations, and can be experienced at Sunshine Meadows. The subalpine zone contains Englemann spruce and subalpine fir trees, and the Lake Louise area is representative of the zone. Douglas fir and grasslands are found in the montane area, which is the least represented and most threatened life zone as a result of increasing development throughout the Bow Valley.

Banff is part of four contiguous national parks, three provincial parks in British Columbia, and several wilderness areas in Alberta. This contiguity assists in, but does not guarantee, the protection of a relatively large undisturbed tract of wilderness that supports a diversity of wildlife, including grizzly bear, mountain goat, bighorn sheep, mountain caribou, Rocky Mountain elk, cougar, and wolves. This entire complex has been recommended by ecologists as the protected wilderness core for a Carnivore Conservation Area because of its potential to provide large-scale wildlife habitat protection.

Visitors to the park should drop in at the Banff Information Centre or Lake Louise Visitor Reception Centre to learn about the park; register for back-country use; and pick up park brochures, including an important one entitled *You Are In Bear Country*. The park has a number of interpretive themes,

A skier pauses in the long ascent up the Wapta Icefield in Banff National Park.

including "Formation and Evolution of Mountain Landscapes"; "Early Man in the Bow Valley"; and "Banff – Birthplace of Canada's National Parks." The Cave and Basin National Historic Site is a must visit.

Parks Canada has identified a number of threats to Banff National Park. Development of sensitive land in the valley bottoms for visitor use is reducing the montane life zone. The potential for a major wildfire is a high risk to people and buildings because natural fires were suppressed for decades, resulting in the unnatural build-up of wood fuel in the forests. Prescribed burns are being used to reduce fuel sources. Poaching and conflicting industrial and tourism developments on adjacent lands threaten park resources. Through amendments to the *National Parks Act* in 1988, Parliament established legal boundaries around Banff townsite and the park's three downhill skiing facilities, beyond which these developments cannot expand.

Banff National Park was added to UNESCO's List of World Heritage Sites in 1985 along with three other contiguous national parks – Jasper, Yoho, and Kootenay. The area comprising the four parks and three adjoining British Columbia provincial parks, Mount Robson, Mount Assiniboine, and Hamber, which were added in 1990, is called the Canadian Rocky Mountain Parks World Heritage Site.

Banff National Park

- **Province: Alberta**
- **Date Established: 1885**
- **Original Name: Rocky Mountain Park**
- **Size: 6,641 square kilometres (2,656 square miles)**
- **Visits: Approximately 4 million per year**
- **Campsites: 2,500 car-based serviced sites in 14 campgrounds**
- **Hiking Trails: 1,500 kilometres** **(900 miles) for day use and back-country hiking**
- **Townsite: Banff**
- **Visitor centre: Lake Louise**
- **Access: Via Trans-Canada Highway, 130 kilometres (80 miles) west of Calgary**
- **Contact: Superintendent, Banff National Park, Box 900, Banff, Alberta T0L 0C0; telephone (403) 762-1500**

One of many similar vistas that take in the clear
waters of Georgian Bay from the Bruce Trail in
Bruce Peninsula National Park.

BRUCE PENINSULA

A landscape of limestone cliffs, wetlands, and woodlots is protected in Bruce Peninsula National Park, one of Canada's newest national parks. The Bruce Peninsula is an 80-kilometre (50-mile) peninsula separating Georgian Bay from Lake Huron. The backbone of both the peninsula and the national park is the Niagara Escarpment, a 725-kilometre (450-mile)-long wall of limestone that winds its way through southern Ontario to Niagara Falls. The national park protects the spectacular and rugged northern end of the escarpment.

Bruce Peninsula National Park represents the ecological features of the western portion of the St. Lawrence Lowlands natural region of the national park system. The 1987 agreement between the federal and Ontario governments creating the park provided for the transfer of Ontario's former Cyprus Lake Provincial Park to the federal government for national parks purposes. It also transferred Fathom Five Provincial Park to Parks Canada, making Fathom Five National Marine Park Canada's first national marine park. To achieve the proposed size of 140 square kilometres (56 square miles), Parks Canada is buying land within St. Edmunds Township from private landowners who are willing to sell their land for park purposes.

The park is a botanist's and zoologist's paradise. Habitats protected in the park support about 40 examples of the over 43 species of orchids found on the peninsula and 20 species of ferns, as well as 300 bird species and a rarely seen population of Massasauga rattlesnakes that remains in swampy and marshy areas. Don't provoke these rattlesnakes; their venom is poisonous.

And don't kill one; park wardens will charge you with endangering wildlife because the rattlesnake is listed as threatened under Ontario's *Endangered Species Act.*

Deer, snowshoe hares, red squirrels, beavers, chipmunks, foxes, and more than a hundred species of breeding birds wander through mixed forest cover of cedar, balsam fir, spruce, birch, and aspen. Geologists also will find much to intrigue them. Karst formations, caves, sinkholes, sheer limestone cliffs, overhangs, sea caves, cobble and shingle beaches make for a fascinating landscape that offers spectacular views of Georgian Bay.

Because of the ongoing land-acquisition program and the relative newness of the national park, it is best to stop in at the Visitor Centre at Little Tub Harbour in Tobermory. Park staff can also direct you to other important natural areas such as the Dorcas Bay Nature Reserve, which was purchased by the Federation of Ontario Naturalists in 1962.

Bruce Peninsula National Park

- **Province:** Ontario
- **Agreement in principle:** 1987
- **Size:** Approximately 80 square kilometres (32 square miles) of the proposed 154 square kilometres (59 square miles) has been acquired from willing sellers.
- **Visits:** Almost 120,000 per year
- **Campsites:** 242 sites in 3 vehicle-accessible campgrounds and 3 remote sites along the Bruce Trail

- **Hiking Trails:** The Bruce Trail, plus several day-hike trails
- **Access:** Highway 6 north from Owen Sound or via the Chi-Cheeman ferry service from Manitoulin Island
- **Local Communities:** Tobermory and Owen Sound
- **Contact:** Superintendent, Bruce Peninsula National Park, Box 189, Tobermory, Ontario N0H 2R0; telephone (519) 596-2233

Bruce Peninsula National Park has two major recreational features. The 730-kilometre (453-mile)-long Bruce Trail, which extends along the Niagara Escarpment from Niagara to Tobermory, reaches its northern end in the park. The views from the trail in the park are breathtaking. Contact the Bruce Trail Association to get a trail map and information on camping and accommodation. A number of trails originate from the Cyprus Lake campground, including one that circles Cyprus Lake and three that extend out to the Georgian Bay shoreline to such places as Overhanging Point, Indian Head Cove, and Halfway Rock Point.

Continued heavy visitor use of this area is having an impact on some of the old cedar forests on the cliff edges. So avoid trampling vegetation and exposed roots and stick to the trail. As well, leave all orchids and wildflowers alone and take care not to disturb other vegetation habitats. Campfires are banned along the shoreline because once a fire starts in the shallow soils, it could destroy in minutes what took nature decades to build. The ban also prevents people from removing more branches from the trees for firewood. Potential water-quality problems are developing at the Cyprus Lake campground and at Dorcas Bay because of recreational developments.

Increased development outside the park in Tobermory and along the shorelines could also threaten park resources in the future if such development continues to expand. To help promote more regional cooperation in protecting the heritage resources of the Bruce Peninsula and other lands, the entire Niagara Escarpment was declared a biosphere reserve in 1990, including the Bruce Peninsula National Park.

Fathom Five National Marine Park, off the tip of the Bruce Peninsula, is a separate protected area that conserves the aquatic resources and several islands in Lake Huron and Georgian Bay and offers excellent opportunities to monitor and interpret the health of the Great Lakes. Park resources include the often-photographed limestone stack of Flowerpot Island, which used to be within the boundaries of Georgian Bay Islands National Park. As well, Fathom Five has more than twenty shipwrecks from the sail and steam transportation eras, plus three lighthouses of historic interest. However, heavy visitor use on Flowerpot Island and intensive diving activity could have a negative impact on heritage resources. Both Bruce Peninsula National Park and Fathom Five National Marine Park make an important contribution to conserving natural areas in the highly developed region of southern Ontario.

CAPE BRETON HIGHLANDS

With the Gulf of St. Lawrence to the west and the Atlantic Ocean to the east, Cape Breton Highlands National Park brings Canadians face to face with their maritime heritage. Located in northern Cape Breton Island, Nova Scotia, the park is characterized by bogs, barrens, forests, mountains, and seashore. Just north of the park, at Aspy Bay, Micmac Indians probably saw John Cabot make his landfall on North America in 1497. The Cabot Trail, which perpetuates Cabot's memory, is flanked by ocean on one side, and the lush forests of the Acadian highlands on the other.

Cape Breton Highlands National Park represents the Maritime Acadian Highlands natural region of the national park system. The park draws its name from the most northerly part of Cape Breton Island, where the highlands dominate the landscape. Cape Breton itself may have got its name in the 1500s from the fishermen of Brittany who resided here.

Cape Breton Highlands National Park is the first park for which land

A wintry seascape seen from the Gulf of St. Lawrence side of Cape Breton Highlands National Park.

Pilot whales are the whales seen most often off the coast of Cape Breton Highlands National Park.

was transferred from a province to the federal Crown for national park purposes. Previously, all national parks were created from lands owned or controlled by the federal government.

Approximately 70 percent of the park is an extensive plateau that rises more than 350 metres (1,150 feet), affording glimpses of some of Nova Scotia's last remaining wilderness. The plateau has been eroded by rivers and streams, producing steep-sided valleys, inlets, and coves. Beaches along the seashore between the headlands have withstood the constant pounding of the sea. Visitors are encouraged to leave their cars on French Mountain and walk the Skyline Trail across a 300-metre (984-foot)-high headland, overlooking the Gulf of St. Lawrence.

Creatures great and small can be sighted with binoculars both within and outside the park. More than 230 species of birds populate the habitats found in this region. Puffins, razorbills, and bald eagles can be seen by boat tour on the Bird Islands, accessible by charter boat that starts an hour south of the park. Whales cruise the waters around the park and are best viewed

from the Cabot Trail lookouts, and on whale-watching tours that leave Cheticamp, Pleasant Bay, Dingwall Bay, St. Lawrence, and Ingonish.

White-tailed deer, black bear, and fox inhabit the lowlands, while moose and small populations of pine marten and lynx are found in the highlands. Fifteen native mammal species are considered endangered, threatened, or rare. A small number of arctic-alpine plants persist as relict populations, widely separated from their current ranges. Plants normally found in Canada's Arctic are found here, as well as in Forillon, Gros Morne, and Mingan national parks, underscoring the unique contribution national parks make to conservation. Many hardwood tree species near their northern limit are found in the park.

Parks Canada offers an extensive interpretation program that every visitor should take advantage of. Some of the interpretive themes include: "Creation of the Highlands"; "The Taiga – Our Arctic-like Land"; "Settlement in Northern Cape Breton"; and "Nova Scotia Wilderness – Rare and Endangered." Visitors to Cape Breton Highlands National Park should also explore other sites of national importance on Cape Breton Island: the eighteenth-century French fortress of Louisbourg; the site of the first wireless station in Canada at Marconi National Historic Site; and Alexander Graham Bell National Historic Site.

Cape Breton Highlands National Park is threatened by a growing number of activities outside the park boundary. Extensive clear cutting around the park has eradicated its major wilderness buffer. Construction of access roads for hydro development, mining, and forestry has also brought human alteration of the environment close to the park. Part of the park was taken away in the Cheticamp area for hydro development in 1956. Action to limit the impact of development on adjacent lands is needed in order to maintain this national park as an important heritage resource in eastern Canada.

Cape Breton Highlands National Park

- **Province:** Nova Scotia
- **Date Established:** 1936
- **Size:** 948 square kilometres (366 square miles)
- **Visits:** Almost 500,000 per year
- **Campsites:** 6 road-accessible campgrounds with about 700 sites, plus 2 back-country campgrounds
- **Trails:** Over 200 kilometres

(124 miles) of hiking trails
- **Local communities:** Cheticamp, Ingonish, South Harbour
- **Access:** Via Cabot Trail
- **Contact:** Superintendent, Cape Breton Highlands National Park, Ingonish Beach, Cape Breton, Nova Scotia B0C 1L0; telephone (902) 285-2270

Sunset over Astotin Lake, Elk Island National Park

ELK ISLAND

Elk Island is one of Canada's oldest and smallest national parks. Created in 1906 to protect a remnant herd of twenty elk, Elk Island National Park is an island of nature in a landscape of grain fields, pastures, industries, and rural communities. The "island" analogy is reinforced by the fact that it is the only national park in Canada that is completely enclosed by a fence. Protected in the park are forests and meadowlands characteristic of aspen parkland. More than 90 percent of this nationally significant landscape has been altered by agricultural use; the balance is threatened.

This national park represents the Alberta Plains component of the Southern Boreal Plains and Plateaux natural region of the national park system. It is an island of rolling transitional aspen parkland with many lakes, ponds, and wetlands, and diverse flora and fauna. Located in the northern section of Alberta's Beaver Hills, the park rises 30 to 60 metres (100 to 200 feet) above the surrounding plains. During the last glacial period, ice melted in place in the Beaver Hills, forming a landscape of hills, hollows, and poorly developed drainage patterns. More than 250 lakes and ponds cover 20 percent of the park. This area was originally called Beaver Hills because of high numbers of beaver living in an ideal habitat.

The possibility that a remnant elk herd would be eradicated by hunting prompted the federal government to create Elk Park as Canada's first wildlife

The quiet beauty of Astotin Lake has drawn visitors to Elk Island National Park since its inception in 1913.

sanctuary. Five men from Fort Saskatchewan petitioned the federal government to create a protected area for the elk. Only after they posted a $5,000 bond to construct a fence around the park was the herd finally protected. Besides elk, plains bison also roam this national park. More than 400 plains bison from the Flathead Indian Reserve in Montana were purchased by the federal government in 1907 and shipped to Elk Island before being delivered to the new Buffalo National Park in Wainwright. About 50 bison evaded capture when the herd was moved to Wainwright, and formed the nucleus of today's plains bison population in the park.

The park is a sanctuary for forty-four kinds of mammals, including moose, deer, lynx, beaver, and coyote. Canada's largest herd of plains bison is protected here, along with a small herd of wood bison. In 1965, wood bison were introduced to the park after an isolated group was found in the Northwest Territories; twenty-four head were shipped to Elk Island National Park and segregated south of Highway 16. Park brochures warn visitors that they are in Bison Country, and remind them to remain in their vehicles and to stay at least 75 metres (250 feet) away from all bison and other large ungulates. If you encounter bison while hiking, don't frighten them, yell at them, or advance on them, and never enter a herd of bison or get between two animals. Give them a wide berth and keep a constant eye on them!

The diversity of aspen and mixed-wood forests, meadows, and wetlands of Elk Island National Park supports more than 230 species of birds, including ducks, gulls, terns, grebes, loons, owls, woodpeckers, and warblers. The endangered trumpeter swan also finds refuge in this wildlife sanctuary, and there is a reintroduction program to ensure its long-term survival. All predators other than coyote, including black bear, grizzly bear, and wolf, no longer live regularly in the park because of its small size. Black bears and wolves have been sighted, but it is believed they are transient and not residents.

Elk Island National Park is threatened by urban development, such as a subdivision and agricultural practices on surrounding lands that may introduce exotic species and pesticides from fertilizers that could impair air and water quality. Because the park is small and fenced, its natural fire cycle, a requirement for maintaining the ecological well-being of aspen parkland, is out of balance. Parks Canada is gradually reintroducing fire into the ecosystem through prescribed burns. Because of a lack of predators, uncontrolled beaver populations are altering natural habitats; however, a more equitable balance between habitats, predators, and beavers is being established.

Visitors can see the various ecological components of Elk Island National Park by using one of the fourteen trails that wander through this important national park. For example, the 2.5-kilometre (1.5-mile) Amisk Wuche trail winds it way through aspen and spruce forests, and crosses wetlands. During the summer months visitors may see some of the 20 to 30 plains bison in the bison paddock north of Highway 16. However, you stand a better chance of seeing some of the over 500 bison that roam free in the rest of the park.

Elk Island National Park

- **Province: Alberta**
- **Date Established: 1913**
- **Size: 194 square kilometres (75 square miles)**
- **Visits: More than 300,000 per year**
- **Campsites: 1 serviced campground has 80 sites**
- **Trails: 14, covering 103 kilometres (64 miles)**
- **Local Communities: Fort Saskatchewan, Lamont**
- **Access: 45 kilometres (28 miles) east of Edmonton on Highway 16**
- **Contact: Superintendent, Elk Island National Park, R.R. 1, Site 4, Fort Saskatchewan, Alberta T8L 2N7; telephone (403) 992-6380**

ELLESMERE ISLAND

Bearded seal, Ellesmere Island National Park Reserve.

A land characterized by ice and snow, Ellesmere Island National Park Reserve also has plants and animals that have adapted to the harsh arctic environment. Dominated by ice, Canada's second-largest national park, roughly half the size of the province of New Brunswick, embodies the characteristics Canadians so commonly associate with the Arctic – a rugged and remote arctic tundra landscape with mountain ranges, ice caps, glaciers, fiords, and fertile arctic oases. Hundreds of glaciers cascade down from arctic ice caps, some extending up to 40 kilometres (24 miles) into valleys and fiords. Mount Barbeau is the highest mountain in eastern North America, at 2,600 metres (8,530 feet). Only a small portion of Mount Barbeau protrudes above the ice cap, and is referred to as a *nunatak*. But south of Mount Barbeau lies Lake Hazen, an arctic oasis that breathes life into this, the most northerly national park.

Ellesmere Island National Park Reserve represents the Eastern High Arctic Glacier natural region of the national park system. It was first announced as a candidate area for national-park status in 1978, and lands were withdrawn from development in 1982 pending the outcome of negotiations between the governments of Canada and the Northwest Territories. In 1986 the two governments signed a federal-provincial agreement, the signing ceremonies taking place on a cold September day at Tanquery Fiord, outdoors, in a stiff chill breeze. The park was formally proclaimed and protected under the *National Parks Act* in 1988.

The national park protects the largest fresh-water lake completely

The polar bear is the largest living land-based carnivore in the world.

Fort Conger was the most northerly permanent building in North America from 1881 until 1950 when the Alert Weather Station was constructed.

north of the Arctic Circle – Lake Hazen, about 80 kilometres (50 miles) in length. Lake Hazen and its surrounding basin capture reflected solar radiation from the Grant Land Mountains, which results in surprisingly warm and long summers and abundant vegetation. Arctic hare sometimes gather in these areas in the hundreds. Thirty species of birds frequent the park reserve area. Small herds of muskoxen and Peary caribou can be seen roaming through the region. The main predators are wolves, arctic fox, and polar bear. Beyond the Lake Hazen shore, the rest of the park is a polar desert, receiving only 6 centimetres (2.4 inches) of rain each year. Southeast of Lake Hazen, a plateau of folded sedimentary bedrock gradually rises to 1,000 metres (3,300 feet) above sea level. Spectacular glacial valleys and fiords such as Discovery Harbour cut into the plateau's uplifted southern rim.

Nomadic peoples (paleo-Eskimo) crossed Ellesmere Island some 4,000 years ago in pursuit of muskoxen as they migrated across northern Canada when it was warmer in this region. The route is now known as Musk Ox Way. The first Europeans to establish a presence on Ellesmere Island were in the British Arctic Expedition of 1875–76. A base was established at Fort Conger in 1875 by the crews of H.M.S. Alert and Discovery, from which they

made sled journeys inland, and across to Greenland. The American Greely Expedition occupied Fort Conger from 1881–83. It served as a scientific, observation, and exploration base. It was also used at different times by Peary from 1898 to 1909 during his various attempts to reach the North Pole. Remains of the building are still standing, but are vulnerable to disturbance.

The ecosystems of Ellesmere Island National Park Reserve have some degree of protection because of their isolation and the lack of adjacent development. However, this exceptionally fragile environment is susceptible to damage from overuse by park visitors, and from the impact of industrial pollutants gathering over the Arctic from Europe. To prevent visitor damage to sensitive features, the park is considering establishing a quota on the number of visitors as a management strategy should the number of visitors warrant it. Parks Canada is also working to remove empty fuel drums and other waste materials that have been abandoned here as a result of various human activities in the area over the last forty years.

Ellesmere Island National Park Reserve

- **Territory: Northwest Territories/Nunavut**
- **Date Established: 1988**
- **Size: 37,775 square kilometres (14,586 square miles)**
- **Visits: 500 per year**
- **Access: Via air charter from Resolute Bay**

- **Contact: Superintendent, Ellesmere Island National Park Reserve, Parks Canada, Box 353, Pangnirtung, Northwest Territories X0A 0R0; telephone (819) 473-8828**

Forillon National Park

■ Province: Quebec

■ Date Established: 1974

■ Size: 240 square kilometres
  (94 square miles)

■ Visits: 175,000 per year

■ Campsites: 3 campgrounds
  with 333 sites

■ Trails: Back country, coastal, plus
  equestrian, hiking, ski, and bicycle

■ Local Communities: Gaspé, Rivière-
  au-Renard, Penouille

■ Access: Via highways 132, 197,
  and 198

■ Contact: Superintendent, Forillon
  National Park, Box 1220, Gaspé,
  Quebec G0C 1R0; telephone
  (418) 368-5505

FORILLON

Forillon National Park protects the end of a long chain of mountains, and the last stretch of land on the Gaspé Peninsula. Located on the tip of the peninsula, on the south side of the St. Lawrence River, Forillon National Park comprises a great diversity of natural habitats. Park visitors can see forests, abandoned fields, sea cliffs, salt marshes, natural prairie, sand dunes, peat bogs, and streams – all within Quebec's first national park.

The contrasting marine and terrestrial environments that support the subarctic and temperate vegetation in Forillon National Park are representative of the Notre-Dame and Megantic Mountains region of the national park system. Forillon is an archaic French word referring to a vertical rocky pillar rising from the sea, a sea stack. One could be seen at the tip of the Forillon peninsula in Champlain's time (1626) until it crashed into the sea in the mid-nineteenth century. The park's interpretive theme – "Harmony between Man, Land and Sea" – illustrates the park's rich natural and cultural history, which has been shaped by the sea that surrounds three sides of the park.

Forillon National Park is located on a mountainous coastal peninsula jutting out into the marine environment, where the Appalachian Mountains disappear into the Gulf of St. Lawrence. Steep limestone cliffs, coves, and shingle beaches are the landscape features that draw so many visitors each summer. Two ancient periods of the planet's geological history are found in the various exposed layers of rocks in the cliffs of Forillon.

The park's vegetation and wildlife are characteristic of the great diversity of habitats protected in Forillon. A mixture of coniferous and deciduous forests covers 95 percent of the park with such tree associations as balsam fir mixed with yellow birch or fir mixed with white birch. There are about fifty different types of tree associations in the park, all influenced by differences in soil, slope, bedrock, weather, and drainage. Although land was cleared over several centuries for farming, fishing remained the major economic activity in this region. The fields are now abandoned, as land farmed by more than 200 families was expropriated to create Forillon National Park.

The Penouille Beach sector of the park contains a number of unique natural communities that are accessible by propane-powered tram. Here lie salt meadows where only salt-tolerant plants grow, and sand dunes. At the nearby interpretive centre, park visitors can learn about the natural history of this interesting sand spit into the Bay of Gaspé. The conservation mandate of Forillon National Park extends almost 150 metres off shore. The coastal area of the park is frequented by whales, seals, and more than 220 species of birds, including gannets, cormorants, kittiwakes, and black guillemots. About ten species of whales, including humpback, minke, fin, and pilot, can be seen from the shores of Forillon. The deep waters off Cape Gaspé harbour schools of small fish that whales such as humpback, minke, blue, and fin feed on, drawing the whales close to shore.

The small and isolated nature of this park, coupled with heavy visitor use and external development pressure, threatens Forillon's ecological integrity. Visitor traffic is exacting a toll on a number of rare species, especially in the peninsula sector. Commercial fishing in the marine sector of the park could also affect the park's biological resources. Beyond the park's boundaries, urban development, poaching, and water pollution in the River and Gulf of St. Lawrence, and forest-management practices on the park perimeter, are having an impact on wildlife habitat and water quality inside the park.

The forests of Forillon National Park
contain the fir and white spruce
typical of the Acadian forest.

The coastline road (shown here around 1950) provides visitors with spectacular views of the world's highest tides.

FUNDY

Visitors can experience the rugged grandeur of the Bay of Fundy's coastline and the solitude of the forests atop the Caledonia Highlands in Fundy National Park. From the park, you can watch some of the highest tides in the world ebb and flow as they carve and sculpt the Fundy shoreline. The landscape is a mixture of broad-leaf and evergreen trees and several peat bogs on top of uplands segmented by deeply cut valleys, all fronting on the tidal shores of the Bay of Fundy.

Fundy National Park represents the Maritime Acadian Highlands natural region of the national park system, an extension of the ancient Appalachian Mountains. The name Fundy comes from either the Portuguese word for "deep" (*fundo*), or the Portuguese or French for "split" (*fenda, fendu*). The bay is both deep and split. The park's name was chosen from among entries in an essay contest held in the New Brunswick high school system.

There are three major interpretive themes in the park: "Fundy Bay and Its Giant Tides," "The Caledonia Highlands," and "Fundy National Park's Cultural History." The maritime Archaic Indians, followed by the Micmac and Malecites, were the original inhabitants of the region. French fishermen and Basques from Spain arrived in the 1500s. Little is known about the pre-European use of the park area. European settlement began in this area only around 1825. The names of park trails, roads, streams, and lakes remind us today of those early settlers. The area was subsequently extensively exploited for its timber, with logging becoming the mainstay of the local economy.

The Acadian forest, a mixed forest, covers most of the park. While red spruce and balsam fir are the dominant species, hardwood ridges of sugar maple and yellow birch provide splashes of gold and crimson in the autumn. Glaciers scoured out depressions, which have filled with mosses and other plants over the centuries, producing peat bogs. The Caribou Plains Trail is a boardwalk that allows you to walk "on" a sphagnum moss mat that is characteristic of peat bog.

Because the shoreline of the Bay of Fundy is along a bird migration

Fundy National Park

- **Province:** New Brunswick
- **Date Established:** 1948
- **Size:** 206 square kilometres (80 square miles)
- **Visits:** About 250,000 per year
- **Campsites:** 4 vehicle-accessible campgrounds provide 600 campsites and 14 backcountry campsites accessible through hiking
- **Trails:** Extensive network, including the 50-kilometre (31-mile) Fundy Circuit
- **Local Community:** Alma
- **Access:** 80 kilometres (50 miles) southwest of Moncton via Highway 114, and 143 kilometres (88 miles) east of Saint John via highways 1 and 114
- **Contact:** Superintendent, Fundy National Park, P.O. Box 40, Alma, New Brunswick E0A 1B0; telephone (506) 887-2000

Water is the dominant physical presence in Fundy National Park: it's in the sodden peat bogs, bubbling streams, swift rivers, and Fundy's surging tides.

route, 187 species of birds have been identified in the park area, of which 100 nest in the park. Some of the common residents include hairy and downy woodpeckers, red-breasted nuthatches, brown creepers, and black-capped and boreal chickadees. Parks Canada has been working to reintroduce a species that disappeared from the skies of Fundy. The endangered peregrine falcon, which was brought close to extinction in eastern North America by the intensive use of DDT in the 1950s and 1960s, was successfully reintroduced to the park and its surrounding ecosystems.

Wilderness-dependent species such as timber wolf, caribou, and American marten were extirpated from the area at the turn of the century as a result of hunting and loss of habitat. However, moose, red fox, bobcat, and black bear can still be found in the park. In the early 1980s, American marten were reintroduced to Fundy. The success of the program is not yet fully assessed, although annual surveys indicate animals in the park and adjacent lands.

Fundy National Park is now a patch of wilderness surrounded by intensively managed forests. On the borders of the park, clear-cut logging and reforestation of these areas with monocultures and non-native species are affecting the diversity and number of animals found in Fundy National Park. Timber operations outside the park are also causing alteration of the park's major watersheds. Fundy's sharp-shinned hawks are experiencing hatching failures due to chemical contaminants in the food chain. The small birds they feed on are exposed to various pesticides throughout the Americas.

To alleviate the growing isolation of Fundy National Park, the Greater Fundy Ecosystem Project was launched to try to manage the park and the surrounding forests on an ecosystem basis. Fundy National Park and the Greater Fundy Ecosystem are also part of a model forest project initiated under Canada's Green Plan to help promote better environmental stewardship of Canada's forests.

The natural beauty of Beausoleil Island caught the
attention of planners and led ultimately to the
creation of Georgian Bay Islands National Park.

Children swim near the park headquarters on Beausoleil Island around 1940.

GEORGIAN BAY ISLANDS

Georgian Bay Islands National Park protects 59 scattered rocky islands, just a small portion of the 30,000 islands sculpted out of the landscape by the last glacial age. The hub of the park is Beausoleil Island, a 7-kilometre (4-mile)-long island that exemplifies the transition zone between northern and southern Ontario characterizing this national park complex. The islands are scattered along a 150-kilometre (93-mile) stretch of the eastern shore of Georgian Bay and provide a unique camping experience on a wild, windswept portion of the Canadian Shield.

This is the land made famous by the landscape paintings of the Group of Seven. During their formative years, these painters focused on the northern Ontario wilderness, including Georgian Bay. Their paintings captured the stark essence of the terrain: the barren rock of the Canadian Shield, jagged coastlines, blue water, and windswept pines. A visit to Georgian Bay Islands National Park brings Canadians face to face with a land etched by ancient glaciers and immortalized by a rich legacy of landscape painting.

The islands in the northern section of the park complex have been heavily glaciated out of the bedrock of the Canadian Shield. The glaciers, and their debris, also produced the sheltered coves, rocky points, and small sand and cobble beaches that draw so many cottagers, boaters, and campers to the edge of the northern Ontario wilderness. To the south of Beausoleil Island, debris from the retreating glaciers was dumped and eventually formed the soil that now supports the lush forests. Here we find one of the best examples of St. Lawrence Lowlands hardwood forests in Ontario. To the north, the forests have developed from a thinner soil base, yet the pines and oaks grow tall and look windswept, clinging with determination to their rocky floors. The transition from the Canadian Shield to southern Ontario can be experienced by visitors to Beausoleil Island.

People are an integral part of Georgian Bay. Over time, Beausoleil Island has been the site for prehistoric hunting and fishing camps and an Ojibway Reserve, and the scene of logging and quarrying activity. The region was once the home of the Huron Indian nation, and later the Ojibwas or Chippewas, who eventually passed it from native ownership to the government through treaty in 1856. Among the islands surrendered were those that are now protected in the national park. The idea of a national park was first proposed in 1920 by Dr. C.B. Orr of the Provincial Museum in Toronto. He called the government's attention to the beauty of Beausoleil Island, which was the largest remaining unsold island held by the trustees of the former Indian lands. During subsequent investigation of the island, other islands worthy of national-park status were also identified. Tourism in the twentieth century resulted in the loss of most of Georgian Bay's islands to private ownership. A petition for protection of the remaining islands resulted in the creation of Georgian Bay Islands National Park in 1929.

Parks Canada wardens conduct a wildlife survey in Glacier National Park. These surveys are essential to tracking the health of park ecosystems.

GLACIER

Flowerpot Island, off the tip of the Bruce Peninsula, was added to the national park a year later after the government acquired it for $165 on the recommendation of a lawyer from Owen Sound, Ontario. (Flowerpot Island is now part of Fathom Five National Marine Park.) Today, Georgian Bay Islands National Park represents both the Central Great Lakes–St. Lawrence Precambrian and the West St. Lawrence Lowlands natural regions of the national park system. The transition zone described above is captured in the two natural regions represented by the national park.

Development pressures on this region of Ontario, a popular tourist destination, are bound to have an impact on park resources. The single largest problem facing Georgian Bay Islands National Park is development outside the park boundary. Pollution from recreational activities, motorboats, and other sources is affecting the water quality of Georgian Bay and, as a result, the park's aquatic environment. Loss of habitat outside the park threatens park species, and acid rain is reducing water quality and could affect species reproduction, possibly reducing the diversity of amphibians and reptiles in the future.

Glacier National Park is a park of sharp contrasts: peaks and glaciers tower over narrow valleys sheltering stands of interior rainforest, and the daunting power of nature reveals itself in the avalanches that roar down steep mountain walls in one of the world's most active avalanche areas. In the summit of Rogers Pass, visitors are dwarfed by the craggy peaks of the Selkirk Mountains, a scene that greeted Major A.B. Rogers when he first identified this pass in 1881 as the route for the railway through the mountains.

The ecological resources of Glacier National Park are representative of the Columbia Mountains natural region of the national park system. The park draws its name from the more than 400 glaciers that cover up to 12 percent of its total area. The Columbia Mountains are older and composed of much harder rock than the Rocky Mountains to the east. The Selkirk Mountains, a chain of the Columbia Mountains, exhibit craggy peaks because the forces of erosion have taken a longer time to sculpt the gneiss rock. Protected in Glacier National Park is one of the largest cave systems in Canada, the Nakimu Caves. It is an extensive system of karst topography, underground passageways, and caverns formed by water that has eroded the limestone.

There are three life zones in the park: interior rainforest, interior subalpine forest, and alpine tundra. Visitors can experience the great cedar and hemlock trees of an interior rainforest, along with ferns and fungi, along the park's Loop Trail. Mountain caribou, grizzly and black bears, and mountain goats are the wildlife most characteristic of this park, although mountain caribou are extremely rare in Glacier today compared to historic populations.

Georgian Bay Islands National Park

- **Province:** Ontario
- **Date Established:** 1929
- **Size:** 25 square kilometres (10 square miles)
- **Visits:** About 65,000 per year
- **Campsites:** 15 campgrounds with a total of 200 sites
- **Hiking:** Extensive trail network on Beausoleil Island
- **Local Community:** Honey Harbour
- **Access:** Via Highway 12 (Midland) and County Road 5 with final access by boat from Honey Harbour
- **Contact:** Superintendent, Georgian Bay Islands National Park, Box 28, Honey Harbour, Ontario P0E 1E0; telephone (705) 756-2415

Researchers put radio collars on one of the remaining few hundred mountain caribou that range in and out of Mount Revelstoke and Glacier national parks.

A rich and diverse bird population that features many neotropical migrants, four species of chickadee, and seasonal invasions of winter finches finds habitats in the park's different life zones.

More than 250 employees of the Canadian Pacific Railway died in Rogers Pass between 1885 and 1916 in a classic struggle of man against the elements. They lost their lives trying to keep the railway tracks free of the snow that continually cascaded down the mountains. But it was the slide of March 4, 1910, in which sixty-two men died, that forced the CPR to abandon its above-ground track, and to construct the Connaught Tunnel through the heart of Mount MacDonald. A large part of the park's interpretive program tells the fascinating story of man, the railway, and the Selkirk Mountains.

Despite the power of nature in the Columbias, the ecological integrity of Glacier National Park is threatened by its small size, the logging of adjacent lands, and the major transportation corridors that fragment the park ecosystem. Key wildlife areas outside the park that support wide-ranging species such as caribou and grizzly bears that migrate across the park boundary are being lost to logging and recreational development. Uncontrolled access to park boundaries has resulted in an increase in poaching. Neotropical migrant birds found in Glacier are threatened by the destruction of tropical rainforests. And the continuing fragmentation and loss of old-growth-forest habitats outside the park threaten a range of old-growth-dependent wildlife including pine martens, woodpeckers, caribou, bats, and owls. The scarce valley-bottom habitats are continually disrupted by the operation of the Trans-Canada Highway and the Canadian Pacific Railway.

Highway traffic and trains represent a constant threat to animal life from large ungulates to small birds.

For the last century, the history of Rogers Pass and Glacier National Park has been one of man trying to control the elements, and to reshape the landscape to support a national transportation route. However, the impacts described above demand a new relationship between human habitation and the natural world if the fragile wildlife that inhabits the steep and harsh valleys of the Columbia Mountains is to survive. If Glacier National Park offers one lesson it is that, despite the formidable nature of the surrounding landscape, the survival of plants and animals in these mountains is a matter of constant struggle. Human pressures serve only to nudge that life into an untenable situation where species loss is a possibility.

Glacier National Park

- **Province: British Columbia**
- **Date Established: 1886**
- **Size: 1,349 square kilometres (520 square miles)**
- **Visits: About 375,000 per year (about 3 million pass through the gates on Trans-Canada Highway)**
- **Campgrounds: 2 main campgrounds provide 78 sites**
- **Trails: 140 kilometres (87 miles)**
- **Local Communities: Golden, Revelstoke**
- **Access: Via the Trans-Canada Highway**
- **Contact: Superintendent, Glacier National Park, Box 350, Revelstoke, British Columbia V0E 2S0; telephone (604) 837-5155**

A remnant of relatively undisturbed mixed-grass prairie near Val Marie and Killdeer is partially conserved in Grasslands National Park.

GRASSLANDS

The prairie grasslands were largely eradicated by human settlements by the mid-nineteenth century. Attempts to protect an undisturbed remnant of this endangered ecosystem have progressed at a snail's pace. Despite numerous political statements of goodwill since 1966, and the signing of two federal-provincial agreements, Grasslands National Park in southern Saskatchewan is only half complete.

Parks Canada has acquired over 420 square kilometres (168 square miles) of the proposed 906-square-kilometre (362-square-mile) Grasslands National Park. Once complete, this park will represent the Prairie Grasslands natural region of the national park system. The object is to establish the first national park that preserves a relatively undisturbed remnant of the mixed prairie grasslands that once covered large areas of North America. Because the government's priority is to acquire land for the park from private landowners who are willing to sell for conservation purposes, park facilities are minimal. So, before planning a visit to Grasslands, call ahead!

The grasslands near Val Marie are a glacial landscape covered with knob and kettle features, meltwater channels, and depressions formed by ice blocks from the retreating glaciers. The "badlands" that characterize some of this area were created, and continued to be shaped, by water and wind erosion. Still surviving in this relatively dry landscape are antelope, mule and white-tailed deer, coyote, and bobcat. Grasslands National Park is a critical haven for numerous species of wildlife whose future is under pressure because of human activities. The park includes the endangered piping plover,

---

Grasslands National Park

- **Province:** Saskatchewan
- **Agreement in principle:** 1975
- **Size:** Currently 420 square kilometres (162 square miles); target is 906 square kilometres (350 square miles)
- **Visits:** Unknown
- **Campsites:** No accommodation in the park
- **Trails:** "Two Trees Interpretive Trail"

- **Local Communities:** Val Marie, Kildeer
- **Access:** Park headquarters is 125 kilometres (75 miles) south of Swift Current via Highway 4
- **Contact:** Superintendent, Grasslands National Park, Box 150, Val Marie, Saskatchewan S0N 2T0; telephone (306) 298-2257

The conservation of relatively undisturbed grassland habitats in Grasslands National Park contributes to the protection of the endangered burrowing owl.

mountain plover, and sage grouse; the threatened burrowing owl, ferruginous hawk, Baird's sparrow, and loggerhead shrike; and the vulnerable black-tailed prairie dogs, Cooper's hawk, long-billed curlew, yellow belly racer, and eastern short-horned lizard.

The lands acquired for Grasslands National Park are of marginal value agriculturally. Nevertheless, some lands were broken for cultivation when farmers first moved into this area after 1906, and the vegetation also has been modified by ranching, the foundation of the social and economic life that developed in this region. If the prairie grassland is to survive, restoration is required

in the absence of traditional natural factors that have caused renewal of the grasslands ecosystem such as grazing bison, natural fires, and thriving wildlife.

The idea of establishing Grasslands National Park was first suggested by the Saskatchewan Natural History Society in 1957. The conditions under which a national park could be established in the Val Marie area were set in 1974: the federal government would not expropriate land for the park; present ranchers could pass on their rights to their heirs; and ranchers wishing to sell would get fair market value. An initial agreement was signed by the federal and Saskatchewan governments in 1981, but it failed to produce a park.

Seven years later, a second, more specific agreement resulted in a successful land-acquisition program that has established half of the proposed park. The federal government has periodically failed to provide adequate funding for land acquisition for Grasslands National Park. After urging from the Canadian Nature Federation, the government did reinstate this land-acquisition budget, maintaining this critical conservation initiative.

The ecological future of Grasslands National Park will require an ecosystem approach. Lands being acquired for the two parks are contained in two blocks, a plan that in no way reflects the ecological realities of the landscape. An ecosystem advisory committee has been proposed. Progress in completing Grasslands National Park is a priority, and Canadians should remain vigilant over government efforts to achieve this national conservation goal.

GROS MORNE

Mountains, fiords, rocky headlands, and broad sandy beaches are the dominant features on Gros Morne, one of Canada's most spectacular national parks, on the east coast of Newfoundland. Both its great natural beauty and its significant geological features prompted the United Nations to add Gros Morne National Park to its List of World Heritage Sites. Visitors to this Newfoundland park can experience a fascinating range of landscapes, from barren highlands to lush coastal forests.

Gros Morne National Park represents the Western Newfoundland Highlands natural region of the national parks system. The dramatic transition from the sandy cobble beaches by the sea to towering rock walls of land-

locked fiords provides a diversity of inspirational vistas. Evidence of successive cultures living in this area dates back thousands of years. The Stone Age people of the Maritime Archaic Tradition lived here some 3,000 to 4,000 years ago. Dorset Culture people inhabited the area over 1,000 years ago.

Some of the rocks found in Gros Morne are found in few other places around the globe. Rocks from the layer that surrounds the Earth's molten core, the mantle, and from the oceanic crust above the mantle, have been exposed by plate tectonics, providing geologists with important clues to the origin of the Earth. These rocks became part of the Earth's crust some 400,000 years ago, but it is not known when they were actually exposed at the surface. There are three life zones in Gros Morne National Park: the sea and the coastline; a long, low coastal plain covered with forests and bogs, cut through by salt-water and fresh-water fiords; and the rugged uplands of the Long Range Mountains to the north and the tablelands to the south.

The Green Garden Trail in the southwestern part of the park provides an excellent hike through several environments. It takes the visitor from a barren landscape lacking vegetation, down into a lush wooded valley, and out to meadows that end at cliffs overlooking the Gulf of St. Lawrence. Giant sea stacks rise from the ocean, standing guard over the rugged coastline. You can descend the cliffs at several places to coves. At the north end of the park rocky beaches and salt flats give way to white sandy beaches backed by sand dunes and grassy fields.

Following the coastline, you pass through several fishing villages that are the backbone of Newfoundland culture, although the current crisis in the Atlantic fishery poses a grave threat to their current survival. Nine communities including Trout River, Rocky Harbour, Sally's Cove, St. Paul's, and Cow Head are human enclaves within the park borders. Government policy

Cliffs soar over Western Brook Pond in Gros Morne National Park. The pond is a fiord that was cut off from the sea by a narrow strip of land and now contains fresh, rather than salt, water.

at the time Gros Morne National Park was first established was to remove such villages. However, few people took advantage of a government relocation program, and federal policy regarding local communities has changed in response to local opposition elsewhere.

The coastal plain gently rises from the coast up to the highlands, passing through several vegetation communities. At low elevation in the valleys of the southern park area are temperate forests of birch, red maple, black ash, eastern white pine, and occasional examples of choke cherry at its most northern extreme. The boreal forest dominates at higher elevation, with balsam fir, black and white spruce, and white birch. This coastal forest is a twisted mat of spruce and balsam fir stunted by wind, spray, and ice, forming what is locally known as Tuckamore or *krummholz*. No matter what the name, it is vegetation that is virtually impassable to hikers. Slicing through the coastal plain due east is one of the most photographed places in Newfoundland – Western Brook Pond, a 16-kilometre (10-mile) land-locked fiord with steep

Gros Morne National Park

- **Province: Newfoundland**
- **Agreement in principle: 1970**
- **Size: 1,805 square kilometres (722 square miles)**
- **Visits: About 120,000 per year**
- **Campgrounds: 5 vehicle-accessed campgrounds provide 287 sites**
- **Trails: 70 kilometres (43 miles)**
- **Local Communities: Rocky Harbour, Cow Head, Woody Point,** Trout River, Wiltondale
- **Access: Southern entrance is 82 kilometres (51 miles) from Corner Brook via the Trans-Canada Highway and Route 430 (Viking Trail)**
- **Contact: Superintendent, Gros Morne National Park, Box 130, Rocky Harbour, Newfoundland A0K 4N0; telephone (709) 458-2417**

cliffs rising nearly 800 metres (2,625 feet). A 3-kilometre (2-mile) hike to the "pond" takes you from the Tuckamore through bogs, and into the boreal forest.

Hiking the Long Range Mountains or climbing to the top of Gros Morne Mountain brings you into the arctic-alpine environment and its stark landscapes. The serpentine rocks of the barren tablelands contain a high percentage of magnesium, which prevents plant growth. Climbing to the top of the tablelands is discouraged in order to protect its natural features.

Threats to park resources include the overuse of Gros Morne Mountain, which has resulted in damage to some of the alpine plant communities that survive here; recreational fishing, which has put Atlantic salmon populations at risk; and logging on lands adjacent to and nearing park boundaries, which is making the back country more accessible. The park contains a variety of wildlife, including woodland caribou, moose, black bear, fox, arctic hare, and populations of arctic and common ferns that may be declining.

Sea kayakers approach Sgan Gwaii, site of the Haida village of Ninstints.

GWAII HAANAS

Gwaii Haanas wilderness archipelago is an internationally significant natural area characterized by a rugged coastline, the San Christoval mountains, one of the finest old-growth temperate rainforests on the west coast of North America, and abundant terrestrial and marine wildlife.

Islands of Wonder and Beauty. Misty Isles. Canadian Galapagos. Moss Capital of the World. Islands at the Edge – these are some of the names given to the collection of 138 islands that stretch out over a 90-kilometre (56-mile) area at the southern end of the Queen Charlotte Islands. This area is part of the ancestral homelands of the Haida people, who call them "Gwaii Haanas," meaning "islands of wonder and beauty." Once threatened by clearcut logging, the terrestrial and marine wonders of this beautiful wilderness archipelago are now preserved in the Gwaii Haanas National Park Reserve.

The plight of Gwaii Haanas was brought to world attention in 1985 when seventy-two Haida were arrested for blockading logging operations on Lyell Island. In 1987 the federal and British Columbia governments signed a memorandum of understanding that ended the logging of this temperate rainforest, and agreed to create a national park reserve covering 15 percent of the Queen Charlotte Islands. To protect the marine environment surrounding these islands, they also agreed to a national marine park that would include approximately 3,400 square kilometres (1,360 square miles) of the waters of the Pacific Ocean and Hecate Strait. The 1987 agreement brought to an end a thirteen-year struggle by the Haida and environmentalists to preserve the magnificent landscapes and seascapes of Gwaii Haanas for future generations.

The biological richness of this wilderness archipelago is exemplified by the fact that it is the only place in Canada that represents three of Parks Canada's natural regions – one terrestrial and two marine. Along with Pacific Rim National Park Reserve, Gwaii Haanas National Park Reserve represents the ecological features of the Pacific Coast Mountains natural region of the national park system. The ecological features of two marine regions of the national marine park system – Hecate Strait and West Queen Charlotte – will be represented in the Gwaii Haanas National Marine Park Reserve.

The true splendour of this national park reserve is derived from its highly dissected mountains, deep fiords, old-growth forests, numerous islands and islets, and the sheer abundance and diversity of wildlife. From the steeply rising San Christoval mountains, which form the backbone of this area, flow streams that feed more than forty fresh-water lakes. Some of the world's largest Sitka spruce, western hemlock, and red cedar trees grow in one of the finest old-growth temperate rainforests that has been left relatively intact on the Pacific coast. Many types of mosses and liverworts proliferate in the moist environment below the forest canopy.

Gwaii Haanas National Park Reserve

- **Province: British Columbia**
- **Agreement in principle: 1987**
- **Original Name: South Moresby**
- **Size: 1,495 square kilometres (577 square miles)**
- **Visits: About 2,000 per year**
- **Facilities: No roads, designated campgrounds, or trails**
- **Local Communities: Sandspit,** Queen Charlotte City, and Skidegate
- **Access: By boat, kayak, or aircraft. Charters available**
- **Contact: Superintendent, Gwaii Haanas National Park Reserve, P.O. Box 37, Queen Charlotte City, British Columbia V0T 1S0; telephone (604) 559-8818**

Bald eagles are a familiar sight on the Queen Charlotte Islands.

Scientists believe that portions of the San Christoval mountains escaped glaciation during the last ice age some 10,000 years ago. These ice-free areas provided refuge for plant and other life, resulting in the evolution of at least thirty-nine species of plants, animals, fish, and insects that are common to this area. The world's largest black bear is the most visible of the seven unique subspecies of mammals that evolved in this, the most isolated archipelago in Canada. There are three indigenous subspecies of birds, including a small saw-whet owl and unique forms of Steller's jay and hairy woodpecker. Three species of beetle are found nowhere else on the planet.

Long before Queen Charlotte was even born, the Queen Charlotte Islands were Haida Gwaii to the Haida, meaning "islands of the people." The Haida are a people born of Haida Gwaii some 10,000 years ago, and they consider Gwaii Haanas a vital part of their spiritual and ancestral home. Recent archaeological research suggests human occupation of Gwaii Haanas dates back 9,000 or 10,000 years. The magnificent Haida totems on Sgan Gwaii, or Anthony Island, serve clear notice to visitors that this area was, and continues to be, a source of artistic and cultural inspiration to the Haida. The stewardship of the Haida over Gwaii Haanas is shared with the government of Canada through the Archipelago Management Board. The board is responsible for the administration and management of Gwaii Haanas, and has equal representation from the Haida and Parks Canada.

Despite its being a largely intact and protected wilderness area on the western edge of Canada, there are still threats to the ecological integrity of Gwaii Haanas. Racoon and rat populations, introduced by man, contribute to the loss of nesting seabird populations through the destruction of eggs and predation of fledglings. Fishing practices have contributed to a loss of marine invertebrates. The introduced Sitka black-tail deer is adversely affecting forest ecology. Visitor use is affecting the heritage resources and features at

Sgan Gwaii, Hotsprings Island, Burnaby Narrows, and Windy Bay; several seabird colonies are also affected.

The totem poles of Sgan Gwaii are a World Heritage Site because of their globally significant cultural value. The natural values of Gwaii Haanas clearly merit World Heritage status and, if so designated, would make this one of only fifteen to twenty areas on the planet designated as a World Heritage Site because of its natural *and* cultural values. Gwaii Haanas has been designated a national park reserve pending the resolution of the dispute over land ownership between the Council of the Haida Nation and the government of Canada.

IVVAVIK

The thundering hooves of the 180,000-strong Porcupine caribou herd bring life to this northern wilderness, tucked into the northwest corner of the Yukon on the border between Canada and the United States. Each new generation of caribou is born here on the coastal plain, now preserved in a wilderness condition within Ivvavik National Park, formerly known as the Northern Yukon National Park.

Migrating over a vast range of 250,000 square kilometres (100,000 square miles), the Porcupine caribou herd is one of the largest in North America, representing some 10 percent of the world's caribou population. Each spring the caribou return to the coastal plain, where their young are born. The discovery of oil at Prudhoe Bay, Alaska, unleashed pressure to build a pipeline through the nursery of the caribou. Ivvavik National Park was created in 1984 to legally protect the calving grounds as wilderness and to

The Firth River cuts through the heart of Ivvavik
National Park.

prevent any industrial development in the area. Ivvavik means "a place for giving birth to and raising young, a nursery."

The ecological features of the Northern Yukon natural region of the national park system are represented in Ivvavik National Park. Creation of this park set a historical precedent in that it was the first time a national park had been established as a result of a land-claim agreement between the government of Canada and aboriginal people. The area was first withdrawn from development in 1978 for the purpose of protecting wildlife and conserving wilderness.

There are three ecological zones in Ivvavik National Park. The arctic coastline has steep coastal cliffs with narrow beaches, spits, and barrier beaches that are 10 kilometres (6 miles) in length and only metres (yards) wide. Deltas that form where rivers flow off the coastal plain provide critical breeding sites and staging and migration grounds for millions of birds.

The coastal plain gently undulates, emerging from the British and Richardson mountains, and slopes toward the Beaufort Sea. Part of the plain was not glaciated during the last ice age. Four major rivers – the Firth, Malcolm, Babbage, and Blow – cut through the plain. The Firth River, with its

gorges and bedrock terraces, is a major route for park visitors. A rich diversity of terrestrial vegetation, such as cotton grass, sedges and mosses, and small areas of birch and willow, is found on the coastal plain, providing important habitat for wildlife, particularly caribou. Aquatic vegetation found in Ivvavik includes bog saxifrage, bladder campion, monks hood, and grass of parnassus, a small grass found in very wet bogs. Compared to the Mackenzie Delta to the east, the number of species in Ivvavik is limited.

Rising above the coastal plain are the British, Barn, and Richardson mountains. The rugged British Mountains are the only large mountain system in Canada that was not glaciated during the last ice age. The most northern extension of the boreal forest extends up the Firth River to within 40 kilometres (24 miles) of the coast. The Richardson Mountains to the east are rounded and much less rugged than the British system. There are elements of taiga, arctic-alpine tundra, and arctic tundra plant communities in this region.

Three major species of bear occur in the northern Yukon region. Grizzly bears use the entire area; polar bears use the coastal plain during the winter, moving out on the sea ice in the summer; and black bears move along the rivers of the Old Crow Flats. Canada's most northerly population of Dall sheep is found in the British Mountains, while the moose habitat extends up to the arctic coast. Golden eagles, rough-legged hawks, snowy owls, gyrfalcons, and the rare and endangered peregrine falcon nest in the mountain habitat.

The coastal plain extends west into Alaska's Arctic National Wildlife Refuge. However, continuing pressure from the U.S. oil industry constitutes a major threat to the ecological integrity of Ivvavik National Park. The caribou calves leave the coastal plain in the Yukon for their post-calving grounds in Alaska, where they find nourishment and refuge from predators. If the U.S. Congress opens up the refuge to development, scientists predict that the Porcupine caribou herd will be decimated. The Canadian government, along with aboriginal and environmental groups in both countries, has been pressing the U.S. Congress for over a decade to legally designate the coastal plain in Alaska as wilderness under the *Wilderness Act*. Parliament invited the United States in 1987 to formally "twin" Ivvavik with the Arctic Refuge for the purpose of jointly protecting this internationally shared wilderness. Congress has yet to pass wilderness legislation.

Ivvavik National Park

- **Territory: Yukon**
- **Date Established: 1984**
- **Original Name: Northern Yukon National Park**
- **Size: 10,168 square kilometres (3,926 square miles)**
- **Visits: About 100 per year**
- **Local Community: Inuvik, N.W.T.**

- **Access: Small aircraft at designated sites, requires permit**
- **Contact: Superintendent, Ivvavik National Park, Western Arctic District, Parks Canada, P.O. Box 1840, Inuvik, Northwest Territories X0E 0T0; telephone (403) 979-3248**

JASPER

Jasper National Park is the largest and most northerly of Canada's four mountain parks. The federal government set aside this area for park purposes in 1907 with the coming of the Grand Trunk Pacific Railway through Yellowhead Pass. Rivers in this area, such as the Athabasca and Miette, were used by early explorers, fur traders, and missionaries travelling the Athabasca Trail between Fort Edmonton and the west coast. The park draws its name from Jasper House, a fur brigade post established by the North West Company around 1813, run by a company clerk named Jasper Hawes. The Jasper House National Historic Site commemorates the role of Jasper House in the fur trade and is located on the Athabasca River below Jasper Lake.

Jasper National Park was first created under the *Dominion Lands Act* as a forest park to preserve the forests of the Rocky Mountains and to protect the rivers and streams that originated in the mountains and crossed the province of Alberta. Today Jasper National Park represents the Rocky Mountain natural region of the national park system, particularly the Front and the Main ranges, two of the three ranges that form the Canadian Rockies. Of the four mountain national parks (Jasper, Banff, Kootenay and Yoho), Jasper is the most representative of this natural region.

There are four life zones in Jasper National Park. Broad river valleys and Douglas fir forests form the montane life zone. Englemann spruce and alpine fir dominate the subalpine forests. Miniature plant life and exposed rocky outcrops constitute the alpine tundra life zone. And the fourth zone, which dominates the scenery, are the glaciers and icefields that flow into the

Mist and evening light play on Mount Kerkeslin in Jasper National Park.

Visitors made use of hired horses and Indian-style tents when they camped in Jasper's Byng Pass in the 1930s.

that protection was needed. Maligne Lake is the largest glacier-fed lake in this part of the Rockies. Medicine Lake, also in Maligne Valley, is part of a karst complex that includes a river that runs under Medicine Lake for 16 kilometres (10 miles), resurfacing in the spectacular Maligne Canyon.

Special geologic remnants of a Devonian reef complex can be seen in the Miette Hot Springs area, located in Fiddle Valley. The exposed rock here was laid down in the Devonian Seas that covered this area some 350 million years ago. The mountain-building process that ended some 40 million years ago raised these sediments to their present height above sea level.

Part of Jasper National Park's educational program focuses on Mount Edith Cavell, its subalpine environment, and the Little Ice Age. Glaciers in this area have receded over the last one hundred years, allowing plant species to recolonize this area. A self-guided interpretive walk provides the

alpine zone. A visit to the following four places will expose the visitor to these life zones: Pyramid Lake to see the montane; Maligne Lake, which is bordered by subalpine forest; the Whistlers near Jasper townsite (accessible by tramway), which is in alpine tundra; and the Icefields Parkway at the Athabasca Glacier, which is the largest glacial icefield in the Canadian Rockies. Travelling from Banff National Park, visitors can reach Jasper by taking the spectacular Icefields Parkway. Many glaciers are visible as you travel from Lake Louise to Jasper Townsite. The highlight of the drive is the 6.5-kilometre (4-mile)-long Athabasca Glacier. Guided tours of the glacier are available. The headwaters of the Athabasca River, part of the Canadian Heritage Rivers System, flow from this natural wonder.

There are a number of natural features in Jasper National Park that contribute to its status as a World Heritage Site. Close to the Jasper Townsite is Maligne Valley. Investigations of this area in 1911 reinforced the perception

Jasper National Park

- **Province: Alberta**
- **Date Established: 1907**
- **Size: 10,878 square kilometres (4,200 square miles)**
- **Visits: Approximately 1.5 million annually**
- **Campsites: 1,750 sites, ranging from fully serviced to primitive, within 10 road-accessible campgrounds**
- **Trails: Extensive network of hiking, snowshoeing, and cross-country skiing trails**

- **Townsite: Jasper**
- **Access: 362 kilometres (220 miles) west of Edmonton via Yellowhead Highway or from Banff National Park via Icefields Parkway**
- **Contact: Superintendent, Jasper National Park, Box 10, Jasper, Alberta T0E 1E0; telephone (403) 852-6161**

visitor with a "window" on how the flora and fauna of North America re-colonized this continent at the end of the last great ice age some 10,000 to 15,000 years ago.

A major portion of the park's montane life zone is found in the Lower Athabasca Valley. While it makes up only 10 percent of Jasper National Park, this zone supports up to 90 percent of the park's wildlife in winter, including elk, sheep, and deer. But this zone is also the focus of development, and includes Jasper Townsite, highway, railway, airport, and utility corridors, campgrounds, and other facilities. Thus, with each new development or expansion, more critical wildlife habitat is lost, and less of the montane life zone is retained for the future.

Like its neighbouring national parks, Banff, Kootenay, and Yoho, Jasper National Park protects extensive tracts of wildlife habitat that are home to elk, moose, deer, mountain caribou, grizzly bear, Rocky Mountain bighorn sheep, wolves, and cougar. An impressive prey-predator wildlife ecosystem is found here in Canada's second-largest national park south of the 60th parallel (only Wood Buffalo National Park is larger).

Poaching and other hunting pressures along park boundaries, coupled with incompatible developments on adjacent lands, threaten park resources. Other threats identified by Parks Canada include continuing road kills of wildlife, the risk of toxic spills along highways and the railway, and the intro-duction of exotic weeds along the Yellowhead Highway. Logging of old-growth forests outside the park's boundary to the northeast is reducing the important habitat of the Rocky Mountain caribou, which migrates across the park boundary. The Foothills Model Forest project is an effort to study ways to better manage the forest resources outside the park to ensure protection for the caribou habitat. It is an example of how protected areas and adjacent lands should be managed jointly to protect natural ecosystems.

KEJIMKUJIK

Kejimkujik National Park encompasses a unique maritime wilderness of tall hemlock forests, interconnected lakes, rivers and streams, and a low rolling landscape. Its rich natural cultural heritage led to its addition to the national park system in 1967. Protected in the park are towering eastern hemlock groves over 300 years old, and nearly 200 of the endangered Blanding's turtle, which are not found anywhere else in New Brunswick. Over 400 petroglyphs depicting traditional Micmac culture and the changes that followed contact with early explorers and settlers are conserved in Kejimkujik.

This maritime wilderness of west-central Nova Scotia is the ancestral home of the Micmac Indians. Ancient names – Peskowesk, Peskawa, Pebble-loggitch – hark back to a nomadic Indian life that was eventually abandoned because government officials encouraged the Micmac to settle on reservations. Kejimkujik's network of lakes and rivers was a major corridor for native people travelling between the forest and the ocean. The name Kejimkujik is one the Micmacs gave to the largest lake in the park. While paddling across it during high winds, they frequently became sore and swollen from crouching in the canoe. Thus the men gave it a nickname, Kejimkujik, meaning "swollen parts."

In sharp contrast to the many national parks in the Maritimes, Keji-mkujik National Park protects an *inland* natural area. The park represents the Atlantic Coast Uplands natural region of the national park system. Many of the park's features are the product of the last ice age. The shallow lakes are depres-sions where the moving ice gouged out the region's rock and soil. The north-west-southeast trending nature of the park's lakes are evidence of the glacier's route. A thin, rocky soil was left behind after the ice retreated. Several rivers

The most extensive collection of petroglyphs drawn by Eastern Woodland Indians in Canada were carved in the soft slate around Kejimkujik Lake.

flow through the park with the most scenic and accessible being the Mersey River, and the more remote West River on the west side of Kejimkujik Lake.

The province of Nova Scotia was interested in creating another national park to complement the Cape Breton Highlands National Park as early as 1945. In 1960 Premier Robert Stanfield reopened discussions with the federal government for a new national park. In 1962 the federal government advised Stanfield that the Kejimkujik area was its preferred candidate, and in 1963 the two governments committed themselves to protect this area. The area was officially protected under the *National Parks Act* in 1974.

Kejimkujik National Park represents a mixed Acadian forest ecosystem that includes hemlock, sugar maple, and yellow birch, which produces a spectacular fall kaleidoscope of colours. It was the forests that first drew people to this region of Nova Scotia. Loggers removed white pine for the masts of ships and red oak for timbers. They moved inland as the coastal forests were

depleted. The forests of Kejimkujik are less than 100 years old; it will take another century or two before a forest similar to the one the late-eighteenth-century loggers found grows back. White-tailed deer are abundant; bear are common; and bobcat and common loons and other waterfowl are protected here. Many amphibians and reptiles, including the rare Blanding's turtle and ribbon snake, are found in the park.

Marten were once widespread in Nova Scotia, but habitat change and trapping eliminated them from the mainland. Since 1987 Parks Canada has released almost 100 American martens into Kejimkujik's softwood forests where they travel through trees and on the ground.

Acid rain is a major threat to this park. The increasing acidity of the park's aquatic environment has an adverse effect on the reproductive rates of fish and amphibians. Parks Canada has been monitoring four lakes since 1978. In fact, the park is one of Environment Canada's research sites to study "long range transport of air pollutants"; it was chosen because of its relatively pristine conditions and unique aquatic environments. A major interpretive message of the park is the impact of acid rain on freshwater ecosystems.

A 22-square-kilometre (9-square-mile) parcel of rugged and beautiful coastal landscape called the Seaside Adjunct was added to the national park in 1988. Parks Canada was excited by this addition, stating that the adjunct "presents a series of stunning contrasts: stark, barren headlands, sheltered coves, and expansive white beaches. Lots of waterfowl and shore birds visit the area, while rolling surf and rock outcrops are home to harbour seals." The Seaside Adjunct is an important breeding habitat for the piping plover. About ten pairs of plovers nest here, a significant portion of Nova Scotia's breeding population. It is hoped that their offspring may help recolonize other areas where the species has disappeared, further enhancing Kejimkujik's significant contribution to Canada's wildlife conservation programs.

Kejimkujik National Park

- **Province:** Nova Scotia
- **Date Established:** 1974
- **Size:** 403 square kilometres (155 square miles)
- **Visits:** About 130,000 per year
- **Campsites:** 1 semi-serviced campground with 329 sites, and 46 primitive campsites
- **Trails:** 14 short walking trails, 60 kilometres (37 miles) of back-country trails, and an extensive canoe system
- **Local Communities:** Within an hour's drive are Lunenburg, Bridgewater, Liverpool, Annapolis Royal, and Bear River
- **Access:** 65 kilometres (40 miles) north of Liverpool off Highway 8. Seaside Adjunct is 25 kilometres (15 miles) west of Liverpool off Highway 103
- **Contact:** Superintendent, Kejimkujik National Park, Box 236, Maitland Bridge, Annapolis County, Nova Scotia B0T 1B0; telephone (902) 682-2772

Kejimkujik Lake is the largest lake in the park of the same name. About 20 percent of the park consists of rivers and lakes.

The timber wolf continues to be numerous in much of its range, but other types of wolves are more or less threatened.

KLUANE

Tucked into the southwest corner of the Yukon, most of the high mountain wilderness of Kluane National Park Reserve is inaccessible except to hardy mountain climbers and intrepid explorers. The park is dominated by the Icefield Ranges of the St. Elias Mountains and by the Kluane Ranges that border the Alaska Highway and Haines Road, presenting a chain of 2,500-metre (8,200-foot) summits.

Massive glacial tongues creep into Kluane's valleys from mountains of ice including Mount Logan, Canada's highest peak, at 5,959 metres (19,550 feet). On the fringe of the icefield is a green belt that forms the eastern boundary of the park and contains alpine meadows, marsh, floodplain, and forests. A dense population of grizzly bears keeps travellers in this area alert!

Kluane means "place of many fish" in the language of the Southern Tutchone people. While Kluane National Park Reserve was not formally established under the *National Parks Act* until 1974, it was first reserved as a national park in 1942. As a park reserve it simply prevented private land holdings from being established. Mining interests were still free to operate. The Kluane Game Sanctuary was created in 1943 to prevent hunting. Mineral interests opposed the proposed park for decades, until they lost a showdown with environmentalists, led by the National and Provincial Parks Association of Canada, in 1972, when the federal government announced its commitment to finally make this national park reserve a reality.

A two-hour drive west of Whitehorse, Kluane National Park Reserve is representative of the Northern Coast Mountain natural region within Canada's national park system. It protects the greatest diversity of Pacific and arctic plant species north of the 60th parallel. The park contains one of the richest wildlife areas in the Canadian north, but because many wildlife species range beyond park boundaries, they are vulnerable to poaching and hunting pressures.

The green belt of the park supports an unusual and varied mix of plants that includes species characteristic of the coast, the Arctic, the western mountains, the northern prairies, and the steppes of Asia. Bluegrass, wheat grass, and sedges form some of the grasslands found in valley bottoms. The valleys also support a montane forest of white spruce, trembling aspen, and balsam poplar. Arctic poppies, purple saxifrage, mountain heather, and moss campion are the robust plants that survive in the alpine tundra, producing a flourish of colour in the summer.

The greatest diversity of birds north of the 60th parallel is found in the southwestern Yukon, including more than 105 species that nest in the park. Rock ptarmigan, wandering tattlers, hawks, owls, arctic terns, peregrine falcons, and golden and bald eagles are a few of many birds that make Kluane their home. Kluane has the largest known concentration of Dall sheep and one of North America's largest subspecies of moose. Hikers are required to take extra precautions in Kluane when hiking in the back country because of the large grizzly bear population.

Even though Kluane's massive mountains and huge glaciers beckon from the Alaska Highway, you cannot reach them by car. However, the Slims River valley penetrates into the St. Elias Mountains and, after a one-way, 27-kilometre (16-mile) hike, visitors arrive at the toe of the Kaskawulsh Glacier. A climb onto the surrounding ridges affords spectacular views of the glacier sweeping around Mount Maxwell. The glacial meltwaters form one of the headwaters of the Alsek River, part of the Canadian Heritage River System,

A rainbow signals the end of a sudden shower where the Cottonwood Trail crosses Victoria Creek in Kluane National Park Reserve.

which flows east, then south, eventually joining up with the Tatshenshini River in British Columbia.

Adjoining the Wrangell–St. Elias National Park in Alaska, these two areas were added to UNESCO's List of World Heritage Sites in 1979, the first joint international nomination ever made. In 1992 the World Heritage Committee also added Glacier Bay National Park and Preserve, which is immediately south of Wrangell–St. Elias in Alaska, to the list. Visitors to this globally significant wilderness can learn about the park through four interpretive themes: "Man in the St. Elias Mountains"; "Life on the Edge of the Icefields"; "Origins of the Landscape"; and "The Ice Fields."

Kluane is designated under the *National Parks Act* as a national park reserve pending the settlement of land-claim negotiations between the government of Canada and first nations peoples of the area. Conservation groups such as the Canadian Nature Federation and the Yukon Conservation Society want the park's boundary in the southeast corner expanded to include that part of the Tatshenshini River that currently flows unprotected through the Yukon. Parks Canada would like to see the boundary expanded to the northwest to include the Klutlan Glacier area. A volcano erupted here some 1,200 years ago, depositing a blanket of white volcanic ash on the glacier's terminus. Amazingly, a white spruce and poplar forest grew here. Moose winter here, and caribou cross the area. There may not be any other place in the world where large mammals live on a glacier!

The ecological integrity of Kluane is threatened by recurring demands for improved visitor access and development of facilities in the back country. In addition, highway traffic and hunting pressure are adversely affecting species such as moose and wolves that migrate out of the park. Organized international poaching also puts park wildlife in jeopardy.

Kluane National Park Reserve

- **Territory: Yukon**
- **Date Established: 1976**
- **Size: 22,013 square kilometres (8,500 square miles)**
- **Visits: Approximately 80,000**
- **Campsites: 1 campground at Kathleen Lake with 41 sites**
- **Hiking: 13 trails, totalling 300 kilometres (186 miles), penetrate various spots along the Kluane Ranges**
- **Local Community: Haines Junction**
- **Access: 160 kilometres (100 miles) west of Whitehorse on the Alaska Highway, or 249 kilometres (150 miles) north of Haines, Alaska on the Haines Road**
- **Contact: Superintendent, Kluane National Park Reserve, P.O. Box 5495, Haines Junction, Yukon Territory Y0B 1L0; telephone (403) 634-2251**

KOOTENAY

Kootenay National Park stretches along the western side of the Continental Divide. It was once described as a "highway park" because of the Banff-Windermere Highway, which runs the entire length of the park. More than 4,500 automobiles travelled this spectacular highway during its first tourist season in 1924. Rugged mountains, glaciated landscapes, canyons, and karst formations characterize this national park, which is part of the 20,160-square-kilometre (8,064-square-mile) four mountain park complex and Canadian Rocky Mountains World Heritage Site.

The headwaters of the Kootenay River gather in this the youngest of the four mountain national parks. The name may come from the Blackfoot Indians, meaning "people of the water." The western side of the Rocky Mountains, including portions of both the Western and west side of the Main Ranges, are represented in the national park system by Kootenay National Park. The Rocky Mountains are composed of three ranges: the Front Ranges to the east, the Main Ranges, and the Western Ranges. To the west of the park

The mountain goats of Kluane National Park Reserve can scramble up the rocky inclines of some of the steepest mountains.

is the Rocky Mountain Trench, which separates the Rockies from the Columbia Mountains.

This part of the central Rockies has served as a north-south travel route since prehistoric times. Pictographs found near Radium Hot Springs at the southern end of the park, where the mountain terrain is more gentle, indicate this area was a meeting place for bands from the plains and mountains. Explorers such as Sir George Simpson and Sir James Hector of the Palliser Expedition had travelled through the valleys and passes of this region. Captain John Palliser concluded that Vermilion Pass would make a good and inexpensive road for "wheeled conveyances."

Construction of the Banff-Windermere Highway was the main catalyst for the creation of Kootenay National Park. A Scottish engineer, Robert Randolph Bruce of Windermere, B.C., promoted the idea of a highway connecting Banff with the Windermere district of British Columbia through Vermilion Pass as a commercial link with the eastern provinces, and a spectacular tourist route. Construction of the B.C. portion began in 1911, but the provincial government could not afford to complete it. The federal government agreed to complete the highway in exchange for the creation of Kootenay National Park. The province gave the federal government ownership of the highway and lands within a belt of 16 kilometres (10 miles) encompassing the highway in 1919, and the park was proclaimed in 1920.

The northern and southern sections of the park are two distinct environments. Driving over Vermilion Pass from Banff National Park, you arrive in the moist and densely forested area north of Kootenay Crossing. A walk along the Fireweed Trail reveals a landscape regenerating after an intense eight-day fire in 1968. Interpretive signs explain the change that fire makes to mountain forests. Engelmann spruce and subalpine fir trees characterize the forests of this area.

The southern portion of the park is not as moist because the air currents flowing from the west lose most of their moisture over the Columbia Mountains. Here the forest is composed of Douglas fir. Wildlife found in the park include elk, mule and white-tailed deer, bighorn sheep, mountain goat, grizzly bear, black bear, and wolf. Mountain caribou, which may have occupied the park in the past, are now absent.

There are a number of points of interest in Kootenay. The carved limestone walls of Marble Canyon, and the mosses and arctic flowers that survive here, are accessible from an interpretive trail. The ochre-coloured Paint Pots were once used by the Kootenai Indians to make vermillion paint to decorate their bodies and teepees. And a four-hour walk takes you to Stanley Glacier.

Wildlife mortality along the Banff-Windermere Highway is a problem, as is the poaching of wildlife, deterioration of back-country areas because of heavy use, and the introduction of non-native plants. Uncontrolled access from adjacent logging roads encourages poachers to prey on park wildlife. However, the park is working on a number of initiatives to enhance protection of its unique heritage resources.

Kootenay National Park

- Province: British Columbia
- Date Established: 1920
- Size: 1,406 square kilometres (543 square miles)
- Visits: 1,850,000 per year
- Campsites: 3 campgrounds provide 401 sites, ranging from fully serviced to primitive
- Trails: 200 kilometres (120 miles) of hiking trails
- Local Communities: Radium Junction, B.C. and Lake Louise, Alberta
- Access: Banff-Windermere Highway (93 South)
- Contact: Superintendent, Kootenay National Park, Box 220, Radium Hot Springs, British Columbia V0A 1M0; telephone (604) 347-9615

KOUCHIBOUGUAC

Kouchibouguac National Park contains a fascinating mixture of natural habitats along Northumberland Strait between New Brunswick and Prince Edward Island. A 25-kilometre (15-mile) system of barrier islands protects the park's warm lagoons and rich salt marshes from the fury of storms and ocean waves. At first glance, the only interesting aspect to Kouchibouguac appears to be its beaches and sand-dune complexes. But protected in this national park is one of the more dynamically changing ecosystems found anywhere in the national park system.

Pronounced "KOOSH-uh-BOOG-oo-WACK," the park's name is that of the river that cuts through the middle of the park. The name is taken from the Micmac expression *Pejeboogwek*, meaning "river of the long tides." Within the national park system, the park represents the New Brunswick lowlands section of the Appalachian Maritime Plain natural region. Much of Kouchibouguac was logged and farmed in the past, leaving the park's forest in an early successional stage of growth.

Three major rivers – the Saint Louis, the Kouchibouguac, and the Black – cut through the park. Over 20 percent of the park's interior is bog because the water cannot drain through the maritime plain. A nature trail takes you to Kelly's Bog, which is more than 5 metres (16.5 feet) deep in sphagnum moss. Moose, deer, black bear, beaver, fox, hare, and coyote inhabit the regenerating forest in the western portion of the park. The Acadian forest throughout the park has black and red spruce, some huge white pines that were spared the axe, and balsam fir.

Shaped and reshaped by ocean storms, winds, and currents, the park's three main barrier islands were formed some 2,500 years ago, and have slowly migrated over the centuries toward the shore. On the edge of the park's forest, fresh water mixes with the sea, forming lagoons that are held back by the islands. A great diversity of plants and animals survives in the lagoons and salt marshes, including resident seabirds and tens of thousands of migratory shorebirds, geese, and ducks. The osprey – the park symbol – and the piping plover nest in the park. One of the largest common tern nesting sites in North America is situated on the park's islands.

A slide show at the Visitor Centre does an excellent job of revealing the various natural habitats you can visit by hiking and canoeing. Park interpretive themes highlight the land-sea interface, as well as the dunes, lagoons, salt marshes, Acadian forest, and regeneration of old fields.

After the governments of Canada and New Brunswick agreed to create Kouchibouguac National Park in 1969, they set about expropriating land and compensating the people who lived within the proposed boundaries of the park. More than a few refused to leave, protesting their forced removal, and occupying the park's administration building on one occasion. After exhausting their legal options, some squatted in the park. The federal government agreed in 1975 to move the park boundary to restore inshore fishing rights, and appointed a royal commission in 1980 to review the situation. Local residents eventually left the park area, but they still retain the right to dock their boats in the park and to remove clams they collect from the Kouchibouguac beaches, as they have done for generations. The federal government has since dropped its policy of expropriating homes for proposed national parks and now works with local people to resolve issues related to new parks.

Park resources are threatened by a number of internal and external stresses. Piping plovers and tern colonies are vulnerable to natural predators and visitor pressure. Sport fishing is adversely affecting brook trout populations, and commercial fishing is reducing populations of clams, fish species, and softshell clams. As a result of the recommendations of the royal commission, commercial fishing is still permitted within the park's boundary, and Parks Canada continues to monitor the health of the park's commercial and non-commercial fish stocks. Research also suggests that forestry operations in headwater areas outside the park may be affecting fish spawning areas.

The ecological complexity of this park, no part of which rises higher than 30 metres (100 feet) above sea level, is remarkable. Long a popular vacation destination, Kouchibouguac deserves to be appreciated for features other than its splendid beach.

Kouchibouguac National Park

- **Province: New Brunswick**
- **Date Established: 1979**
- **Size: 239 square kilometres (92 square miles)**
- **Visits: About 175,000 per year**
- **Campsites: 2 main campgrounds with 240 drive-in sites and 9 walk-in sites. There are also 3 primitive camping areas.**
- **Hiking: Park is unique because of its 25-kilometre (15-mile) bicycle pathways, 13 nature trails, and 30 kilometres (18 miles) of cross-country ski trails**
- **Local Communities: Kouchibouguac Village, Richibucto, Pointe-Sapin, Saint-Louis-de-Kent, Rexton**
- **Access: Located 100 kilometres (62 miles) north of Moncton or 110 kilometres (68 miles) south of Bathurst via Highway 11**
- **Contact: Superintendent, Kouchibouguac National Park, Kouchibouguac, New Brunswick E0A 2A0; telephone (506) 876-2443**

More than 20 percent of Kouchibouguac's interior is low-lying bog.

Visitors to La Mauricie National Park study an interpretive display that explains the formation of Lac Wapizagonke and other topographical features.

LA MAURICIE

La Parc national de la Mauricie protects a maple and spruce forest dotted with almost 150 lakes and ponds in the heart of Quebec. The province's largest national park, La Mauricie encompasses a landscape of low, rounded hills that are the billion-year-old Laurentian Mountains. La Mauricie sits on a transition zone where the boreal forest of the Canadian Shield merges with the mixed forest of the St. Lawrence Lowlands. In autumn, the sugar maples, yellow birch, and beech paint the landscape in a kaleidoscope of brilliant colours.

La Mauricie represents, within the national park system, the ecological features of the Canadian Shield, the Quebec Laurentians, and the St. Lawrence Lowlands. Bounded by two large rivers, the Mattawin to the north and west and the Saint-Maurice to the north and east, the park is named for the river to the east, which was itself named for the Sieur Maurice Poulin de la Fontaine in the eighteenth century. Beaver, moose, red fox, snowshoe hare, and black bear remain the main inhabitants of this land.

The names of lakes and rivers in La Mauricie speak of the cultural heritage of Canada's founding peoples. These forests were home to native people up to 5,000 years ago. The French who settled here encountered the Attikameks, a nomadic people with the same origins as the Cree and Algonquin, who travelled the rivers and forests, hunting game and gathering roots and berries. More than thirty archaeological sites from prehistoric times have been found on the banks and islands of lakes Wapizagonke, Caribou, and Anticagamac. Logging began in the area as early as 1831, and with the construction of hydroelectric power facilities between 1898 and 1903, the region became a major pulp and paper centre.

Three large natural corridors, faults in the earth's crust that have been worn away by the last glacial age, lie within the park and are the focus of recreational activities. Cutting across these corridors in the southern part of the park is a major parkway that was constructed after the park was established. One of the park's major features is Le Passage at the northern end of Lac Wapizagonke. Through here passed glaciers, caribou and moose, nomadic hunters, trappers and lumberjacks, sport fishermen, and, today, canoe-campers in search of the wild outdoors of La Mauricie.

La Mauricie is among the more ecologically isolated national parks in Canada. Like other natural environments, the park is affected by air pollution, global warming, and destruction of the ozone layer. Its territory is relatively small, and its ecosystems extend beyond its boundaries, so they are more or less directly affected by different forms of resource exploitation practised outside the park, such as hunting, trapping, logging , and agriculture. And heavy visitor use in the summer is straining park resources.

The impressive natural features of this Laurentian landscape are now protected in La Mauricie National Park because there was strong local and political support for conserving them. Resolutions from numerous municipalities and chambers of commerce were received by the minister in charge of national parks in 1969. And a conference of mayors of municipalities in central Quebec called on the Quebec government to support the creation of a national park in the valley of Rivière Saint-Maurice. Backed by local support, the minister of national parks, the Hon. Jean Chrétien, member of Parliament for Saint-Maurice, reached agreement with the Quebec government on the creation of La Mauricie National Park in August 1970.

La Mauricie National Park

- **Province: Quebec**
- **Date Established: 1977**
- **Size: 536 square kilometres (207 square miles)**
- **Visits: About 300,000 per year**
- **Campsites: 3 semi-developed campgrounds, with 518 campsites, plus 181 primitive sites on canoe routes**
- **Trails: Numerous canoe routes, short hiking trails**

- **Local Communities: Shawinigan, Grand Mère, Saint-Jean-des-Piles, and Saint-Gerard-des-Laurentides**
- **Access: 70 kilometres (43 miles) north of Trois Rivières via Highway 55**
- **Contact: Superintendent, La Mauricie National Park, C.P. 758, 465, 5th Street, Shawinigan, Quebec G9N 6V9; telephone (819) 536-2638**

MINGAN ARCHIPELAGO

The Mingan archipelago is a unique set of limestone islands located off the north shore of the Gulf of St. Lawrence between Ile Anticosti and the Quebec mainland. They are spread out in a 175-kilometre (108-mile) chain that extends from Longue-Pointe to Aguanish, Quebec, lying, on average, 4 kilometres (2.4 miles) off the Quebec shore. Forty main islands in this forty-seven-island archipelago were acquired by Parks Canada in 1983 from Dome Petroleum of Calgary.

The Mingan Archipelago National Park Reserve represents the geomorphology, and flora and fauna of the eastern portion of the St. Lawrence Lowlands natural region of the national park system. There is no general agreement with respect to the origin of the name "Mingan." It is a Montagnais word for "wolf" as well as a Breton word for "rounded stone," which pretty much describes the islands' topography.

The federal government has wanted to protect the Mingan archipelago as part of the national park system since 1926 because of the natural attractions and recreational potential of the islands, which then were still uninhabited and largely in primeval condition. In 1943 the National Parks Bureau wrote that "while we are planning post-war park development for Quebec province and Canada as a whole, serious consideration should be given to the acquisition of these islands."

The main "natural attractions" of the Mingan archipelago are the monoliths, rock arches, and grottoes that were formed by wave action, ice, and the natural chemical reactions between water and limestone. Uplifted

Park staff talk to visitors about the unique topographical and other features of the Mingan Islands.

millions of years ago, the limestone islands of the Mingan are distinct from the Canadian Shield, and have been shaped and carved into some magnificent natural sculptures. On these island beaches visitors can explore the largest concentration of arches and sea stacks in Canada.

Two distinct climatic systems come together in the Mingan archipelago, producing a diversity of vegetation that is unique in Quebec. A temperate maritime climate covers most of the islands and with the cold surrounding waters produces tundra-like vegetation. This climatic mixture, along with the limestone bedrock and beach deposits, supports six distinct vegetation communities.

Over 60 percent of the islands are covered by forests, with fir stands being the predominant plant community, and black and white spruce occupying the rest. Peat bogs cover almost 20 percent of the islands, supporting the largest number of plant communities. The harsh climate on the edge of the sea has produced a moorland habitat with low plant formations of lichen and shrubs that cover 10 percent of the archipelago islands. The remaining communities are found on the cliffs, and are fresh-water and salt-water marsh habitats. The arctic-alpine vegetation found at this latitude is rare in North America. Almost 500 vascular plant species are found in this park, some of which are usually found 4,000 kilometres (2,500 miles) to the north or in the mountains to the west.

The archipelago also supports a great diversity of bird life, with at least 200 species of birds having been sighted here. Gulls, terns, and kittiwakes nest on the shorelines, moors, and cliffs of the islands, including one cliff where more than 1,000 black-legged kittiwakes gather. The park symbol is the puffin, which is also found here. Up to 100,000 common eiders spend the winter on the archipelago. Over 4,000 individuals from a different subspecies nest on the park islands. The discharge of fresh-water rivers into the archipelago waters creates a diversity of marine habitats. Nine types of whales visit this area, including the minke whale.

Park resources are threatened because there is unrestricted access to the islands. As a result, ecologically significant environments have been trampled, and birds have been disturbed during nesting seasons. Emphasis is being placed both on increased surveillance of sensitive areas and on improved visitor awareness of fragile ecosystems. Visitors should acquaint themselves with sensitive park resources so that they do not become part of the problem. External threats to park resources include water pollution in the St. Lawrence River, and the possibility of spills from shipping.

The Mingan Archipelago is the first national park reserve established outside the Yukon and Northwest Territories. The Parliament of Canada declared it a national park reserve under legislation in 1984, pending the settlement of the aboriginal land claim of the Attikamek-Montagnais. The Mingan Band Council sits on the Management Council with Parks Canada to advise on the planning and management of the park reserve.

Mingan Archipelago National Park Reserve

- **Province:** Quebec
- **Date Established:** 1984
- **Size:** 150 square kilometres (58 square miles)
- **Visits:** About 25,000
- **Campgrounds:** Primitive campsites on some islands
- **Access:** Archipelago accessible only by sea
- **Local Communities:** Havre-Saint-Pierre, Mingan, Longue-Pointe-de-Mingan
- **Contact:** Superintendent, Mingan Archipelago National Park Reserve, P.O. Box 1180, 1303 Digue Street, Havre-Saint-Pierre, Quebec G0G 1P0; telephone (418) 538-3331

Purple mountain heather flourishes in the subalpine meadows of Mount Revelstoke National Park.

MOUNT REVELSTOKE

Purple mountain heather flourishes in the subalpine meadows of Mount Revelstoke National Park.

Located on the western slopes of the Selkirk Mountains, Mount Revelstoke National Park encompasses the Clachnacudainn Range and a large icefield that is the source of several turbulent streams that flow out of the park. Along with Glacier National Park, which lies 16 kilometres (10 miles) to the east, Mount Revelstoke represents the Columbia Mountains natural region of the national park system. The smallest of the western mountain parks, Mount Revelstoke is considered the "little sister" of Glacier, and includes many of the same ecological features.

Mount Revelstoke is named for the city of Revelstoke located to the east of the park. The city itself was named for Lord Revelstoke, the head of a British bank that helped finance construction of the Canadian Pacific Railway.

The formation of a local mountaineering club in Revelstoke, B.C., in 1910 sparked events that led to the creation of the park. The club succeeded in getting the City of Revelstoke to build a hiking trail from the city to the summit of Mount Revelstoke. Because the mountain attracted a large number of visitors, pressure was exerted on Parliament in 1912 by local representatives of Revelstoke to construct a road to the summit, and to designate the area a dominion park. The federal order creating Mount Revelstoke National Park in 1914 drew attention to the "glaciers, mountain peaks and waterfalls which attract large numbers of tourists and make it adapted for the purposes of a scenic park."

The Mount Revelstoke Summit Parkway, completed in 1927, is one of the few places in the national park system where visitors can literally drive to the top of a mountain and into subalpine meadows. However, the growing popularity of this drive has resulted in damage to the meadows, and has threatened alpine vegetation. Travelling the parkway from the Trans-Canada, you can see the changes from the rainforest in the valley to the spectacular flowers of the subalpine. Inspiring views of the Selkirk and Monashee mountains, as well as the Columbia and Illecillewaet valleys, greet the visitor at the summit.

The vegetation and wildlife found in Mount Revelstoke National Park are very similar to those in Glacier National Park. Stands of temperate interior rainforest, interior alpine forests, and alpine tundra characterize the landscape as you move from the valleys to the mountains. Mountain caribou, grizzly and black bears, mountain goats, and small mammals such as a variety of bats and rodents are protected in Mount Revelstoke National Park.

Visitors to Mount Revelstoke can learn about the park's work to protect the disappearing caribou. The size of Mount Revelstoke and Glacier national

HRH Prince of Wales stands beside a tablet he unveiled in September 1919 to celebrate the construction of the road to the mountain summit.

parks is inadequate for the wide-ranging woodland caribou. In addition, the continuing fragmentation of old-growth forests through the region is thought to contribute to the decline of caribou because they spend a lot of time in old-growth forests at all elevations and during all seasons. Parks Canada and the B.C. Forest Service are working together to determine what habitat must be protected to ensure the survival of the woodland caribou.

By focusing on the natural resources that are representative of the Columbia Mountains, and the resource-management practices necessary to conserve these resources, the message of Mount Revelstoke National Park is that society needs to protect ecosystems that surround parks and not just the parks themselves. Visitors are encouraged to learn about the condition of park resources through park interpretive programs, and about what steps are being taken to preserve Canada's smallest mountain national park.

Mount Revelstoke National Park

- **Province: British Columbia**
- **Date Established: 1914**
- **Size: 260 square kilometres (100 square miles)**
- **Visits: About 125,000**
- **Campgrounds: Two back-country campgrounds**
- **Trails: 40 kilometres (24 miles) and 15 kilometres (9 miles) for cross-country skiing**

- **Access: Trans-Canada Highway**
- **Local Community: Revelstoke**
- **Contact: Superintendent, Revelstoke National Park, Box 350, Revelstoke, British Columbia V0E 2S0; telephone (604) 837-5155**

NAHANNI

Persistent allusions to the "Headless Cave," "Funeral Range," and "Deadman Valley" drop a veil of mystery around the canyons and valleys of this northern wilderness. The backbone of Nahanni National Park Reserve is the 300 kilometres (186 miles) of the South Nahanni River and the four canyons protected within this ribbon-like park. Nahanni appears to have several meanings. One is "people of the west" in Athapaskan. Another is that the early inhabitants of this area were known as "Nahannis," meaning "people over there far away."

Snuggled up against the southeast border of the Yukon Territory, Nahanni is characterized by turbulent rivers, rugged mountains, caves, canyons, and hot sulphur springs. The focal point of visitor interest in Nahanni is Virginia Falls, where the South Nahanni tumbles over a 92-metre (302-foot) precipice, twice the height of Niagara Falls.

The natural features of the Mackenzie Mountains natural region are represented in the national park system by Nahanni. The jagged peaks of the Ragged Range Mountains rise above the northwestern edge of the park. The upper reaches of the South Nahanni River are slow, and meander through tundra-capped mountains. Just below Virginia Falls, rapids and whirlpools characterize the river as it quickly passes through Fourth Canyon. Further downstream from "Hell's Gate," or "Figure Eight Rapids," is a 90-degree river bend with large standing waves, back eddies, and cliff faces. Third Canyon, "The Gate," is an impressive narrowing of the river guarded by Pulpit Rock below 213-metre (699-foot) vertical cliffs. The most easterly canyon was

The beaver is the only mammal that can build

a dam in the waters of the Nahanni National

Park Reserve without contravening the *National*

Parks Act.

The creation of Nahanni National Park Reserve put an end to a proposal to build a dam for hydroelectric purposes at Virginia Falls.

untouched by glaciers during the last glaciation and has walls that rise over 1,100 metres (3,610 feet).

Vegetation in the park is characterized by boreal species such as spruce and poplar in the lower valley bottoms, and alpine tundra in the mountains. Sensitive or endangered wildlife is protected within the boundaries of Nahanni, including Dall sheep, grizzly bears, trumpeter swans, mountain goats, and peregrine falcons. More than 120 species of birds have been identified.

There is more to Nahanni's wilderness than the South Nahanni River. There are many hot springs within the park, the largest being Rabbitkettle Hotsprings, Kraus Hotsprings, and Hole-in-the-Wall Hotsprings. Some spectacular karst landscapes, such as Grotte Valerie, are represented in the park.

Nahanni National Park Reserve

- **Territory: Northwest Territories**
- **Date Established: 1976**
- **Size: 4,765 square kilometres (1,840 square miles)**
- **Visits: About 1,500 per year**
- **Campsites: A number of primitive campsites; dry sandy or cobble beaches are also recommended as camping locations.**
- **Hiking: Several developed trails and portages (Rabbit Kettle, Virginia Falls, Sunblood Mountain, and Figure Eight Rapids)**
- **Local Communities: Fort Liard, Nahanni Butte, and Fort Simpson**

- **Access: Chartered float planes are usual mode of access. No motorized craft permitted for recreation in the park. Liard Highway from Fort Nelson provides road access to Blackstone Territorial Park, which is 64 kilometres (40 miles) from the eastern park boundary.**
- **Contact: Superintendent, Nahanni National Park Reserve, Bag 300, Fort Simpson, Northwest Territories X0E 0N0; telephone (403) 695-3151**

Grotte Valerie is a 2-kilometre (1.2-mile) collection of passages formed by percolating water that has modified the limestone. This cave system is believed to be older than 350,000 years, and it is decorated with hundreds of small but still-growing stalagmites and stalactites.

Nahanni National Park Reserve was the first site added by UNESCO to its List of World Heritage Sites, which started in 1978. The park merited this international status because of its extensive canyon system, Virginia Falls, its remarkable karst terrain, and its many hot springs. The first World Heritage plaque in the world was posted at Virginia Falls in 1979.

As part of future land-claim negotiations with aboriginal people, Parks Canada may secure boundary extensions in three key areas: the Ragged Range to the northwest; the karst area north of First Canyon; and the Tlogotsho Plateau. The addition of these areas would improve the park's ability to represent the Mackenzie Mountains natural region.

There are several significant threats to the heritage resources protected in Nahanni National Park Reserve. The park's water quality could be threatened by a potential lead/zinc mine on Prairie Creek that runs into the South Nahanni River. The inactive tungsten mine on the headwaters of the Flat River is also being considered for redevelopment as an international tourism resort and convention centre. And visitors are putting pressure on the wilderness quality and experience of the park. Even though Nahanni has relatively few visitors, visitor use is heavily concentrated on the river corridor within a compressed period of two months.

The park is designated a national park reserve under the *National Parks Act* pending the settlement of a land claim between the government of Canada and aboriginal people in the region. Native people from Nahanni Butte hunt, fish, and trap wildlife in the park, which contributes food, hides, and raw materials for craft production.

North Baffin Island

Over 22,200 square kilometres (8,880 square miles) of arctic wilderness was withdrawn from development in April 1992 for the purpose of creating a national park on northern Baffin Island. Both the government of Canada and the Tungavik Federation of Nunavut, the latter representing the Inuit of the eastern Arctic in land-claim negotiations, agreed to create the national park as part of the Nunavut land-claim agreement. While the park may not be formally established until 1996 because of the need for further negotiations, both parties are committed to creating the park. The land withdrawal ensures that the lands will be protected until the park is formally protected under the *National Parks Act.*

Under the terms of the Nunavut agreement, the federal government and the Inuit must negotiate within three years an Inuit impact and benefit agreement that will provide for training, employment, business opportunities, and park access. The federal government then has one year to formally establish the park.

The new national park will represent land, vegetation, and wildlife of the Eastern Arctic Lowlands natural region of the national park system. The marine and terrestrial features of this national park are also of international significance. North Baffin Island National Park includes three separate land areas: almost all of Bylot Island, the lands around and including Oliver Sound, and a large area on the Borden Peninsula. Steep cliffs over 300 metres (990 feet) in height on Bylot Island support large colonies of seabirds including some of the largest populations of thick-billed murres and black-legged kittiwakes in Canada. Bylot Island also contains habitats that support gyrfalcons, ivory gulls, peregrine falcons, sandhill cranes, and arctic terns. Over 20 percent of Canada's breeding population of greater snow geese are found in the lowlands of southwestern Bylot Island.

The dominant characteristic of Eclipse and Oliver sounds are deeply cut fiords and glaciers that descend to the sea, providing spectacular views for hikers and kayakers. Treeless lowlands covered each summer with colourful arctic wildflowers, lichens, and sedges are found in the Borden Peninsula section of the park, providing food for birds and other wildlife. Bylot Island and its surrounding sea ice are inhabited by polar bears, while small herds of caribou can be found on Baffin Island. A number of marine mammals, including narwhals, belugas, walrus, killer whales, and five species of seal live offshore. The endangered bowhead whale also inhabits the waters of this area.

Local Inuit residents continue to practise their traditional way of life, which includes hunting and fishing activities. Inuksuit and old campsites, as well as more than fifty sites representing pre-Dorset, Dorset, and Thule cultures, are found in this area. Of great scientific interest are the dinosaur bones that have been uncovered on Bylot Island.

North Baffin Island National Park

- **Territory: Northwest Territories/Nunavut**
- **Date Established: Lands withdrawn for park purposes in 1992**
- **Size: 22,252 square kilometres (8,592 square miles)**
- **Facilities: None**
- **Local Communities: Pond Inlet, Arctic Bay**
- **By kayak and air**
- **Contact: Superintendent, Eastern Arctic, Parks Canada, P.O. Box 1720, Iqaluit, Northwest Territories X0A 0H0; telephone (819) 979-6277**

Horizontal strata are exposed in magnificent cliff sections along the shores of Admiralty and Elwin inlets on the northern Borden Peninsula section of North Baffin Island National Park.

This area is a virtual Arctic oasis with an unusually high biological productivity. It is a major wildlife corridor, staging area, and breeding site. For example, over 80 percent of North America's narwhal population either migrates through or spends its summers in Lancaster Sound, and over 50 percent of Canada's entire eastern Arctic population of marine-dependent birds migrate, nest, or feed here. The ecological values of Lancaster Sound must be protected from potential industrial accidents. Action is still required in this region to establish a national marine park to protect the fragile marine ecosystem contained in Lancaster Sound to the north of Baffin and Bylot islands.

PACIFIC RIM

Pacific Rim National Park Reserve is a thin strip of land that extends for 150 kilometres (93 miles) along the west coast of southern Vancouver Island. The powerful forces of the Pacific Ocean meet the Sitka spruce, red cedar, and western hemlock old-growth forests that still stand along the rim of the continent. Waves crash against the craggy headlands or roll up the sandy beaches in this spectacular national park reserve that is dedicated to the wilderness and coastal heritage of Vancouver Island.

Pacific Rim National Park Reserve represents the Estevan Coastal Plain portion of the Pacific Coast Mountain natural region of the national park system. It has three separate units: the Long Beach section to the north; the Broken Group Islands section in the middle; and the West Coast Trail section to the south. Because of its small, narrow land base, Pacific Rim does not include a complete ecosystem or watershed in either the Long Beach or the West Coast Trail component. The Broken Group Islands, however, form an intact west-coast archipelago.

The most northerly unit is named for the 11-kilometre (7-mile) stretch of surf-swept sand called Long Beach. Here the visitor can explore the four life zones of the park: subtidal, intertidal, foreshore, and forest. The subtidal zone covers the underwater area, which is part of the federal government's national marine park system. Kelp beds extend from the surface down as far as 30 metres (100 feet). At special interpretive programs, park staff bring up sea life for visitors to see. Grey whales migrating between the Arctic Ocean and Mexico pass by the park, making for some exciting whale-watching experiences from mid-March to mid-April. Information about this and other park

phenomena is available from the Wackaninnish Visitor Centre or the park Information Centre.

The tide pools of the intertidal zone are exposed at low tide. Brightly coloured sea anemones, starfish, and seaweeds are visible in the rocky areas of Long Beach. Florencia Bay at the south end of the Long Beach unit is one place to explore the intertidal zone.

The extensive sand beaches, with their sparse plant life and sprawling logs, characterize the foreshore, which is a transition zone between the intertidal and forest zone. Walk the Rain Forest Trail and experience the red cedar and western hemlock trees of this fully mature, temperate rainforest.

The Broken Group Islands is made up of more than 100 islands and islets in Barkley Sound covering an area of about 60 square kilometres (24 square miles). People can explore a number of islands by boat, but only eight islands have designated campsites. These islands are popular with paddlers. Parks Canada will soon be implementing a reservation system here, similar to the West Coast Trail, to prevent overuse and environmental degradation.

The West Coast Trail was first laid out in 1890 as a telegraph line. But in January 1906, the passenger ship s.s. *Valencia* crashed onto a rocky reef. Rescuers on shore and aboard other vessels could not reach the ship for two days, leaving 126 passengers and crew to perish. As a direct result, between 1907 and 1912, a team of sixty men built a life-saving trail along a portion of the Vancouver Island coastline that was known as the Graveyard of the Pacific. The West Coast Trail that hikers walk today was therefore originally a route through the dense forest that shipwrecked sailors could use to reach coastal communities. Maintenance of the trail after the Second World War was sporadic, and eventually abandoned due to improvements in navigational aids and maritime technology.

Public interest in reviving the trail was launched in the 1960s by several

Lush temperate rainforest greets hikers at the
north end of the West Coast Trail.

groups, including the Sierra Club of Western Canada, that pressed for the creation of Pacific Rim National Park Reserve. This rugged hiking trail, intended for experienced back packers only, switches from extensive hard-packed sand beaches to rocky headlands and racing surge channels. Hikers are required to reserve a permit for hiking the trail from Parks Canada. The Nitnat Triangle is an important addition to the park and is a good area for canoeing.

The ecology of Pacific Rim National Park Reserve has been assaulted by industrialization from all sides. Logging adjacent to the park could adversely affect park resources, watersheds, and wildlife. As well, the long-term impacts of the January 1989 oil spill are as yet unknown.

Pacific Rim is designated as a national park reserve pending the settlement of a land claim between the government and the First Nations people who have lived here for thousands of years.

Pacific Rim National Park Reserve

- **Province: British Columbia**
- **Agreement in principle: 1970**
- **Size: 286 square kilometres (110 square miles)**
- **Visits: Almost 800,000 per year**
- **Campsites: Long Beach Unit has 2 campgrounds, 94 drive-to sites, and 80 walk-in sites. The Broken Group Islands has 8 designated primitive campsites. The West Coast Trail has primitive campsites throughout its length.**
- **Trails: 8 hiking trails plus the** 75-kilometre (46-mile)-long West Coast Trail
- **Local Communities: Tofino, Ucluelet, Bamfield, Port Renfrew**
- **Access: Long Beach via Highway 4 from Port Alberni; West Coast Trail via trailheads at Port Renfrew and Bamfield; Broken Group Islands by boat from Ucluelet, Bamfield, Toquart Bay**
- **Contact: Superintendent, Pacific Rim National Park, Box 280, Ucluelet, British Columbia V0R 3A0; telephone (604) 726-7721**

POINT PELEE

The sandy tip of Point Pelee National Park marks the most southerly mainland point in Canada. Point Pelee is a dynamic, 17-kilometre (10-mile) sand peninsula with long beaches shaped by storms and the fluctuating water levels of Lake Erie. Pelee stretches farther south than the northern California border and the northern Mediterranean countries in Europe. The park's low latitude coupled with the moderating effects of Lake Erie produce a local climate that supports a great diversity of plants and animals, species typical of the Carolinian life zone that reach their limit in southwestern Ontario. Some of the woodland flowers of Point Pelee are the first to be seen in Canada in spring because of the relatively warmer climate.

A unique mixture of marsh, forest, sand dunes, and beach, Point Pelee represents the western zone of the St. Lawrence Lowlands of the national park system. The park is obviously named for the spit that extends into Lake Erie. In French, *pelée* means "bald" or "denuded," a description given to the peninsula in 1670 by Fathers Dollier and Galinée. Pelee is a young landscape: most of it was formed between 4,300 and 1,200 years ago from sand that was deposited some 10,000 years ago along a ridge that extended across the bottom of Lake Erie to the American shore. The park's impressive beach-dune complexes support a diversity of plants and animals representative of the Carolinian forest of southern Ontario. The habitat of the prickly pear cactus is protected in the grasslands and savannahs of Point Pelee, and is found in few other places in eastern Canada.

The western part of the park is a complex landscape of old dune ridges and beaches, while the eastern part is a rather simple barrier beach. These two areas enclose a 1,080-hectare (2,700-acre) marsh that covers just over 65 percent of the park area. The fresh-water marsh supports many species of plants, including swamp rose mallow, and is designated a wetland of international significance under the Ramsar Convention for International Wetlands. A kilometre (0.6-mile)-long boardwalk takes park visitors out into the splendour of the marsh. If you visit the park in July or August, make sure you stop at the Marsh Cart at the beginning of the boardwalk to learn about life in the marsh, marsh ecology, and the need for proper stewardship of this heritage resource.

If you are going to visit Point Pelee in May, get there early. This is birding season, and sometimes so many birders are in the park to see the spring migration that the park's visitor parking lot is full by 7:00 a.m. on weekend mornings. More than 350 species of birds have been sighted here; of these, about one hundred nest in the park and almost fifty reside over the winter. The central Mississippi and eastern Atlantic flyways overlap near

Chief warden Norris McCarron points out the park's attractions to visitors in 1957.

Pelee, and birds searching for food touch down here much to the pleasure of the binoculars-carrying birders. And from late August to early October, monarch butterflies gather here to migrate south to Mexico. Daily counts sometimes reach into the thousands.

Because much of the Carolinian forest has been altered in southern Ontario, including in Point Pelee, many species are rare. In the park, seventy species of vascular plants, twenty-five bird species, eight butterfly species, seven fish, two amphibians, and three turtle species are "rare" in Ontario, with a large number officially listed by the Committee on the Status of Endangered Wildlife in Canada as rare, threatened, or endangered. Habitat loss, over-exploitation, and other factors have eliminated nine of thirty recorded reptile and amphibian species, as well as the southern flying squirrels. Nearly 40 percent of all vascular plants in the park are not native to the park. While some can out-compete native species, others are isolated plantings that are being

Point Pelee National Park

- **Province: Ontario**
- **Date Established: 1918**
- **Size: 15 square kilometres (6 square miles)**
- **Visits: almost 500,000 per year**
- **Campsites: There is no camping in Point Pelee, but motels, private campgrounds, and bed-and-breakfast guest accommodation are located close to park.**

- **Hiking: A number of day-use and interpretive trails**
- **Local Community: Leamington**
- **Access: 10 kilometres (6 miles) south of Leamington**
- **Contact: Superintendent, Point Pelee National Park, R.R. 1, Leamington, Ontario N8H 3V4; telephone and TDD (519) 322-2365**

The Marsh Boardwalk extends more than a kilometre (half mile) into the marshland that is the heart of Point Pelee National Park.

removed under the park's Ecosystem Management Program. This work is funded by a local association of volunteers, the Friends of Point Pelee.

Given the extent to which land outside the park has been manipulated, and the stresses exacted by large numbers of park visitors and historical manipulation of park resources, it is no surprise that the threats to the Point Pelee ecosystem are extensive. However, since 1985 the visitor impacts due to birding have been reduced because the amount of off-trail use has declined dramatically. So don't trample the vegetation if you are going birding in the fragile natural environment of Point Pelee; learn about the park's "Protect Pelee's Plants" program before setting out to any of the park's attractions. Approximately 11 percent of the dry land area in the park is devoted to visitor facilities, which represents a decline from earlier years.

The park's Ecosystem Management Program addresses many of these stresses. Its white-tailed deer no longer have natural predators due to the extirpation of top carnivores, with the result that deer browse on rare Carolinian vegetation. The herd was reduced several years ago, and an immuno-contraceptive was tested in 1993 with the objective of achieving a better balance between deer and park vegetation so that the forest can regenerate naturally. In April 1993 the southern flying squirrel was reintroduced to the park after an absence of fifty years. And the Natural Habitat Restoration Program actively promotes the planting of native Carolinian trees on public lands throughout Essex County.

The various interpretive programs and self-guiding trails provide park visitors with tremendous opportunities to learn about one of Canada's most endangered ecosystems. However, the park also has a lot to tell about how it is trying to stabilize and restore the Carolinian life zone. Look for these messages. They underscore the notion of protected areas as islands of hope, and the importance of individual action.

The ingenious imposter Grey Owl and his wife, Anahareo, welcome visitors to their cabin on Lake Ajawaan. His pet beavers, Jelly and Rawhide, entered the cabin through the woodpile on the right.

PRINCE ALBERT

Prince Albert National Park protects a natural transition zone spanning the boreal forest to the aspen parkland and fescue grassland. Here the plants and animals from three different life zones create a diverse mosaic. And, because much of the land surrounding Prince Albert has been developed for agriculture or forestry, the park is an important refuge for the rich diversity of wildlife in this region of transition.

The Southern Boreal Plains and Plateaux natural region of the national park system is represented in Prince Albert National Park. The park's overall landscape is rolling, dotted with large lakes such as Waskesiu, Crean, and Kingsmere and hundreds of smaller ones. The gently undulating terrain and waterways were created by the advance-and-retreat of the glaciers during the last ice age, some 10,000 years ago.

The change from boreal to aspen parkland occurs gradually from north to south. In the northern part of the park, lakes, ponds, streams, and bogs are found in a mixed forest. Coniferous species predominate, but many deciduous species such as aspen and birch occur as well. The Boundary Bog interpretive trail takes the visitor into a black spruce muskeg to learn about the natural history of this zone. Sphagnum moss and reindeer lichen can be found in many places. Grasslands mix with trembling aspen trees in the aspen parkland section of the park. About one-quarter of Canada's remaining natural fescue grasslands are protected in Prince Albert National Park.

One of the many important conservation roles of the park is that it maintains the second-largest, and only fully protected, nesting colony of the white pelican in Canada. The area is protected within a special Preservation Area so that the colony will not be disturbed by people, but there are opportunities to glimpse these magnificent birds elsewhere in the park. The park also protects the natural habitat for plants and animals representative of grasslands, parklands, and the boreal forest, such as badger, ground squirrel, otter, lynx, wolverine, elk, moose, deer, and black bear. A small herd of woodland caribou wanders through the area, which also contains wolf denning areas. And almost 100 plains bison roam free in Prince Albert National Park.

The rich history of Prince Albert National Park is well documented in a book by Bill Waiser, entitled *Saskatchewan's Playground: A History of Prince Albert National Park*. The creation of Prince Albert National Park appears to be a classic example of political wheeling and dealing. Before agreeing to nominate Mackenzie King as their candidate to Parliament in 1926, the Prince Albert riding association presented a list of demands to King, including a request for a national park. After defeating a young lawyer and future prime minister

---

Prince Albert National Park

- **Province: Saskatchewan**
- **Date Established: 1927**
- **Size: 3,875 square kilometres (1,496 square miles)**
- **Visits: About 180,000 per year**
- **Campsites: 6 vehicle-accessible campgrounds provide 521 sites, plus 62 back-country sites**
- **Trails: Extensive network of back-country and front-country trails for**

hiking, mountain biking, and cross-country skiing.

- **Access: 70 kilometres (43 miles) north of Prince Albert via scenic Highway 263**
- **Visitor Centre: Waskesiu Lake**
- **Contact: Superintendent, Prince Albert National Park, Box 100, Waskesiu, Saskatchewan S0J 2Y0; telephone (306) 663-5322**

A summer thundercloud approaches the reed-ringed shores of one of the many lakes protected in Prince Albert National Park.

named John Diefenbaker, Prime Minister Mackenzie King presided over the opening of Prince Albert National Park in 1928.

The cabin in which Grey Owl lived is maintained on Lake Ajawaan. Grey Owl wrote numerous books and articles, and assisted in the production of wildlife films focusing on the preservation of the beaver, which was the symbol of his crusade to conserve wildlife in Canada. Grey Owl was employed by the National Parks Branch in 1931 to promote a broader interest in conservation. Not until 1938, after his death in a Prince Albert hospital, did the public learn that Grey Owl was, in fact, Archibald Belaney, born in England.

Prince Albert National Park faces a number of management issues. For example, fire suppression over the years may have thrown the natural fire cycle out of balance, producing a different forest community than might exist if wildfires had been allowed to burn. Overfishing and the manipulation of water levels has caused major declines in walleye and lake trout populations. The lack of a buffer around the north end of the pelican nesting area, and future logging in the area, may threaten its long-term viability. Prince Albert National Park is part of the federal government's Model Forest Program, which may lessen some of the potential impact of logging of adjacent lands.

Visitors to Prince Albert National Park can learn about this park through some of its major interpretive themes, which include: "Boreal Wilderness Values"; "The Transition from Northern to Southern Canada"; "Landscapes of the Southern Boreal Plains"; and "Grey Owl." Prince Albert National Park is also part of an international research program to monitor changes in the natural environment caused by global climate change.

Grass and water in Prince Edward Island National Park.

PRINCE EDWARD ISLAND

Prince Edward Island National Park is among the smallest of Canada's national parks, but size is deceiving. The park protects a wonderful diversity of landscape features, including extensive barrier spits, long sandy beaches, coastal sand dunes, meadows, ponds, and forests. The red sandstone cliffs that are interspersed between the beach areas give this thin strip of nature on the north shore of Prince Edward Island its rugged and picturesque nature.

Ecological features of the Maritime Plain natural region of Canada, as identified by the national park system, include beaches, dunes, salt marshes, warm lagoons, and remnants of the Acadian forests. The park takes its name from the province in which it is located. Originally called Ile St-Jean by the French, it was named Prince Edward Island in 1799 after the Duke of Kent, father of Queen Victoria.

The first public call for this national park was made in 1923 by the member of Parliament for Queens. While the Dominion Parks Branch was sympathetic to the suggestion, it had no money. Progress in the mid-1930s on the proposed Cape Breton Highlands National Park in Nova Scotia and Fundy National Park in New Brunswick prompted action in Prince Edward Island. In

More than 100,000 visitors simmered on the beaches in 1950 when this photograph was taken. A decade later, the park was attracting ten times that number.

1936, the path for the national park was cleared when the federal government allocated funds for the project, and the provincial government approved legislation to expropriate the land required. Prince Edward Island National Park, initially consisting of 8 square kilometres (3.2 square miles), was formally proclaimed in 1937. The park has proven immensely popular: the number of visitors rose from 108,000 in 1951 to over a million in 1962. It remains one of the most frequented national parks, receiving 750,000 visitors every year.

Prince Edward Island is a landscape of transitions. Standing on one of the boardwalks installed to protect the dune ecosystem and its fragile vegetation, you can see the different ecological zones. Rising above the sea and the beach are sand dunes, formed over time by sand particles deposited by the wind. Marram grass begins to grow, holding the sand in place against the wind and sea. Farther back from the sea, you can see how other forms of vegetation, such as shrubs and trees, have taken hold, eventually leading to a spruce forest growing on tertiary dunes.

Look for the *krummholz* effect – short, twisted trees that mark the transition from the sand dune to forested ecosystems. They are continually assaulted by the wind from the sea, producing their gnarled look and longer branches on the down-wind side. Behind the dunes are *barachois* ponds, where the shifting sands have closed off salt-water inlets from the sea, or fresh-water outlets from the land, creating a land-locked pond that is replenished by rain-water and streams. This is a very productive habitat for fish, plants, birds, and insects. Over 256 species of bird have been recorded along the beach, cliffs, and inland at Prince Edward Island National Park, including common and arctic terns, black guillemots, osprey, and the endangered piping plover. Wildlife species include red fox, coyote, snowshoe hare, mink, muskrat, and racoon. There are two cultural sites worth a visit in Prince Edward Island National Park: Green Gables House, and Dalway by the Sea or Dalway

House. Green Gables House, near Cavendish, was the setting for author Lucy Maud Montgomery's *Anne of Green Gables*, which was first published in 1908. Dalway House is a landmark in the eastern part of the park, an example of Victorian architecture and of the opulent summer homes built by rich citizens. The original portion of the house was erected in 1896 by Alexander MacDonald of Cincinnati, a director of Standard Oil.

Prince Edward Island National Park poses many challenges to park managers. Coastal dune environments like this are very dynamic, and subject to great changes. Facilities installed to allow visitor use are often affected by shifting dunes. Previous attempts to manage the coastal erosion processes have caused many changes to the coastlines. Visitor pressures are causing the loss of avifauna colonies such as terns and piping plovers, and the loss of vegetation in campgrounds. Before setting out, visitors must learn about the park's various fragile environments and how to minimize the impact of their visit.

Much of Prince Edward Island is devoted to agricultural land use. The use of fertilizers, pesticides, and insecticides is having a negative effect on park resources such as shellfish and wildlife because of the runoff from farmlands. Coastal deposition processes in the park and elsewhere are also affected by the dredging of harbour mouths to provide access to the sea for fishing boats. The number of internal and external impacts on the resources of Prince Edward Island National Park points to the difficulty in trying to maintain a coastal strip of wilderness that is used intensively for recreation, and surrounded by heavily modified landscapes.

PUKASKWA

Pukaskwa is the largest national park in Ontario. The theme of the park is "Wild Shore of an Inland Sea." The wild shore is where the wrinkled and worn Canadian Shield meets Lake Superior, the inland sea. A park brochure sets the mood for a visit to this northern Ontario wilderness: "A remote and unyielding wilderness where man is and forever will be only a visitor." The land and the seashore, populous with a mixture of black flies, mosquitoes, deer flies, and sand flies, allows you to relive the days of early explorers.

Pronounced "PUCK-a-saw," the park's name is of uncertain origin. It could mean "fish-cleaning place." In 1971, the government of Ontario first agreed to create a national park protecting 80 kilometres (50 miles) of the Superior shoreline. It was not until 1978 that the lands were officially transferred to the federal Crown. In creating the park, the federal government confirmed that the traditional rights of the Robinson-Superior Treaty Group would be upheld in the park. The federal-provincial agreement also confirmed that Ontario Hydro could maintain and operate a powerline through the park.

Prince Edward Island National Park

- **Province: Prince Edward Island**
- **Date Established: 1937**
- **Size: 22 square kilometres (8.5 square miles)**
- **Visits: About 750,000**
- **Campgrounds: 3 campgrounds provide 570 sites**
- **Trails: Day-use and interpretive trails**
- **Local Communities: Cavendish, North Rustico, Brackley, and Stanhope**
- **Access: 24 kilometres (15 miles) north of Charlottetown via Highway 15**
- **Contact: Superintendent, Prince Edward Island National Park, 2 Palmers Lane, Charlottetown, Prince Edward Island C1A 5V6; telephone (902) 566-7050**

The White River, part of which flows unprotected outside Pukaskwa National Park, runs swiftly through a narrow gorge before its entry into Lake Superior.

The White River, part of which flows unprotected outside Pukaskwa National Park, runs swiftly through a narrow gorge before its entry into Lake Superior.

Pukaskwa represents some of the least impaired natural resources found within the Central Boreal Uplands natural region of the national park system. Underlain by the thin soils of the Canadian Shield, this wilderness environment is a transition zone from a boreal to a southern hardwood forest. Plant species characteristic of the arctic and alpine life zones are found along the harsh Lake Superior shoreline. Rare plants, including the Pitcher's thistle and Franklin's lady's slipper, are protected within this park.

The survival of the most southerly caribou population in Canada, numbering no more than forty individuals, is one of the major resource challenges in Pukaskwa National Park. Habitat change and predation are causing a decrease in this remnant population. A major cause of habitat change is fire suppression. The boreal ecosystem inhabited by the caribou is typically influenced and renewed by fire. Fire will have to be used to retain this ecosystem. Wolves, moose, black bear, and bald eagles are also found here.

The highest point in the park is Tip Top Mountain, which towers some 455 metres (1,492) feet above Lake Superior. But there is no trail to this point. The major back-country experiences to be had in Pukaskwa include the Coastal Hiking Trail, which extends along the Lake Superior shoreline from Hattie Cove to the North Swallow River. However, before embarking on your trip, make sure you register with the park Visitor Centre and get an update on hiking conditions.

Or you can canoe the Superior shoreline from Marathon to Michipicoten Harbour outside of Wawa. But this is a potentially dangerous trip, as terrifying storms and fogs can appear in a matter of minutes. Expect to be grounded one-third of the time because of the Superior wind. There are also a number of day hikes that can be enjoyed on a self-guiding interpretive trail to Hattie Cove–Horseshoe Bay–Halfway Lake that start out of the main campground.

The wilderness of Pukaskwa is threatened by acid rain and possibly by intensive land uses outside the park's boundaries. Forestry operations on adjacent lands, exploration and development of mineral resources, and proposed hydroelectric developments could adversely affect park resources. Parks Canada has nominated the national park as a potential biosphere reserve for the purpose of generating a more systematic ecosystem approach to preserving the natural buffer around Pukaskwa National Park.

Pukaskwa National Park

- **Province:** Ontario
- **Agreement in principle:** 1971
- **Size:** 1,878 square kilometres (725 square miles)
- **Visits:** About 20,000 per year
- **Campsites:** 1 serviced campground provides 67 sites
- **Hiking Trails:** 60-kilometre (37-mile)-long Coastal Hiking Trail, plus day-use trails in the Hattie Cove area
- **Local Communities:** Heron Bay, Marathon
- **Access:** 325 kilometres (200 miles) northeast of Thunder Bay via Highway 627 from Trans-Canada Highway
- **Contact:** Superintendent, Pukaskwa National Park, Highway 627, Hattie Cove, Box 39, Heron Bay, Ontario P0T 1R0; telephone (807) 229-0801

Many of the roads in Riding Mountain National Park were built during the Great Depression by men working on unemployment relief projects.

RIDING MOUNTAIN

A rugged landscape west of Lake Manitoba, Riding Mountain National Park is the meeting place of three ecological zones on the Manitoba Escarpment. Canada is fortunate that early action was taken to establish Riding Mountain National Park to protect this meeting place because, today, it is an island of nature amidst a sea of agriculture. The park is important to the region because it protects the headwaters of thirteen area watersheds, which have been heavily modified right up to the park boundary.

Riding Mountain National Park represents the natural features of the Southern Boreal Plains and Plateaux region of the national park system. The eastern part of the park also includes some natural features of the Manitoba Lowlands natural region of the system, which is immediately to the east of Riding Mountain. Along with the escarpment, rolling forested hills, meadows, lakes, and streams are the most dominant physical characteristics in this park.

The Manitoba Escarpment is a highland plateau, and is known locally as Riding Mountain. The highest point in the park is, at 756 metres (2,480 feet) the third-highest point in Manitoba. The mountain may have got its name from Indian pack trails that were used by early explorers of this region. However, as Henry Youle Hind of Trinity College, one of the first white men to explore this region in 1857, discovered, the Indians of this area refused to climb Riding Mountain itself as it was "full of devils."

The lands constituting Riding Mountain National Park were first reserved in 1906 as a federal timber reserve. By 1927, numerous resolutions from a number of city and town councils and rural municipalities were urging the federal government to establish a national park in the Riding Mountain Forest Reserve. In February 1928, the legislative assembly of Manitoba passed a resolution calling on the federal government to establish national parks in the vicinity of Riding Mountain *and* eastern Manitoba, but the federal government was prepared to create only one park. Further studies of the Whiteshell area in eastern Manitoba, which was originally withdrawn for park purposes in 1928, left the federal government unimpressed. A favourable report on the Riding Mountain area, coupled with strong support, resulted in the creation of Riding Mountain National Park in 1929.

The park encompasses three life zones: eastern deciduous forest, aspen parkland, and boreal forest. The eastern deciduous zone dominates the park's eastern zone with its Manitoba maples, bur oak, elm, and ash trees. The park protects one of the last stands of eastern deciduous forest in Manitoba.

The open fescue grasslands amid stands of aspen and mixed boreal forest in the central part of Riding Mountain National Park are characteristic of the aspen parkland area. Waterfowl, fish, and bird species inhabit the many

Riding Mountain National Park

- Province: Manitoba
- Date Established: 1929
- Size: 2,973 square kilometres (1,148 square miles)
- Visits: About 400,000 per year
- Campsites: 6 vehicle-accessible campgrounds provide 700 sites
- Trails: 11 back-country trails with primitive sites
- Visitor Centre: Wasagaming

- Local Communities: McCreary, Onanole
- Access: 225 kilometres (140 miles) northwest of Winnipeg via Highway 10
- Contact: Superintendent, Riding Mountain National Park, Wasagaming, Manitoba R0J 2H0; telephone (204) 848-2811

prairie potholes and lakes that are found in this zone, "holes" that were left behind when the glaciers retreated and the ice melted.

The boreal forest zone is found in the northern part of the park where you can see the spruce trees overtaking the aspen parkland. The Brulé Trail takes visitors through a burned area, revealing the importance of fire as a natural agent of renewal in boreal and prairie ecosystems. However, the park's natural fire cycle is out of balance, in part because fires are suppressed to prevent damage to the surrounding communities. Such suppression has a negative impact on fire-dependent species in the boreal zone.

The predominant mammals in Riding Mountain National Park include black bears, wolves, elk, moose, white-tailed deer, and beaver. There are also hibernation dens for the red-sided garter snake, and nesting habitats for turkey vultures and the great grey owl. Recent studies confirmed that the black bears found in Riding Mountain are among the largest in the world. However, because the bear habitat extends outside the park, and roads and development have encroached upon the park boundary, bears are being lost to hunting and poaching.

Other developments are having a negative impact on park resources. For example, exotic plant species and noxious weeds from adjacent agricultural activities, and from cottages inside the park, have been introduced into the park and are competing with native species. Wind-blown agricultural chemicals are also affecting the park. Tourism and recreational development both inside and outside Riding Mountain are having an effect on Clear Lake. Recent research suggests that the lake water has an extremely slow turnover rate. Pollutants may not be as quickly "flushed" from this lake as it was once thought. Further research and less development are required.

Riding Mountain National Park and its surrounding region was designated the Riding Mountain Biosphere Reserve in 1986 under the Man and the

Prickly rose brightens a patch of green in Riding Mountain National Park.

Biosphere Program of the United Nations. The purpose of the biosphere program is to promote a balanced relationship between the people and the natural environment through research, education, and practical conservation projects. In Riding Mountain, attempts are being made to coordinate the activities of the national park, which is the "core" protected area of the reserve, and the twenty-five surrounding municipalities, which are in an area identified as a "zone of cooperation." It is hoped that cooperation between the park and surrounding communities will ensure the long-term survival of the nationally significant natural values found in both the park and the surrounding region.

ST. LAWRENCE ISLANDS

Despite being Canada's smallest national park, St. Lawrence Islands National Park makes a contribution to the national park system no less significant than that of any other national park. It protects in a natural state islands that are representative of one of the most beautiful river landscapes on the North American continent. The northern extension of several species, such as the pitch pine and shag-bark hickory, is protected in the park. And the habitat for the rare black rat snake, as well as for other varieties of amphibians and reptiles, is sheltered from development on the park's twenty-three islands and numerous islets.

Visitors pose in the Mallorytown picnic shelter in 1904 — the year St. Lawrence Islands National Park opened.

Ecological features that are representative of several natural regions of the national park system are found in St. Lawrence Islands National Park. The park is located in the Central Great Lakes–St. Lawrence Precambrian natural region, and adjoins both the west and central sections of the St. Lawrence Lowlands natural region. Hence, this park is a transition zone for flora and fauna. A remarkable diversity of plant life grows on these granite islands that are scattered over 80 kilometres (50-miles) in the St. Lawrence River.

The Thousand Islands are actually the peaks of an ancient and now worn-away mountain range that connected the southern edge of the Canadian Shield with the Adirondack Mountains in upper New York State. Called the Frontenac Axis, this land bridge became a chain of islands after the glaciers retreated and the flowing waters of the St. Lawrence River were established. The park landscape is dominated by deciduous, broad-leafed trees, interspersed with open fields that were once cultivated but are now abandoned. An incredible number of plants can be observed in the park, such as Dutchman's breeches, hepatica, spring beauty, trout lily, and white trillium. Nesting wood peewees, warblers, ospreys, herons, migrating ducks, flickers, brown creepers, and white-breasted nuthatches are among some of the bird life that can be observed.

The St. Lawrence Islands National Park is situated in a great inland waterway studded with up to 1,700 islands, known to early explorers as "Les Milles Iles," or the Thousand Islands. These lands were surrendered in 1856 by the Mississauga Indians under treaty and held in trust by the government of Canada, and were eventually sold for summer homes. However, when the federal government designated several of the larger islands for sale in the early years of this century, local residents petitioned the government to retain them for public use. In 1904 the lands were transferred from the control of the superintendent general of Indian affairs to the minister of interior for "park

A Parks Canada gate attendant welcomes visitors to St. Lawrence Islands National Park.

purposes." They were formally protected as national parks under the *Dominion Forest Reserves and Parks Act* in 1914.

The ability of St. Lawrence Islands National Park to fully protect ecosystems representative of this natural region is limited by its small size and the fact that the islands are widely dispersed. Outside pressure on park resources is sure to have an impact on the park's fragile resources. The Thousand Islands is a popular holiday retreat and summer playground. The resulting recreational use is compacting soil and damaging vegetation on the islands, and affecting shoreline habitats for plants and wildlife. Park resources are also subject to air, water, and noise pollution from land and water traffic, agricultural practices, waste disposal, and the use of pesticides by shoreline communities. The spillage of petroleum and other products from commercial freight and pleasure craft using the St. Lawrence River could have an adverse effect on the shoreline environment of the park.

The ability of Parks Canada to maintain the ecological integrity of

Canada's smallest national park is limited because its jurisdiction and authority stop at the water's edge. However, through a number of resource-monitoring projects, rehabilitation of overused areas, and education and public relations programs aimed at visitors and neighbouring communities, the government hopes to increase local awareness that St. Lawrence Islands National Park is of national and local importance. In these ways, park officials are attempting to take a leadership role in protecting the key ecosystems of the upper St. Lawrence River.

TERRA NOVA

Remnants of the ancient Appalachian Mountains and a boreal landscape are protected in Terra Nova, Canada's most easterly national park. Over 200 kilometres (120 miles) of rugged shoreline with rocky headlands, cliffs, coves, and cobbled beaches are the product of the last glacial age. The North Atlantic Ocean penetrates the park in three areas – South West Arm, Newman Sound, and Clode Sound – giving the park its main interpretive theme, "Sheltered Seas Touching Boreal Landscapes." One of the park's most distinctive features is the fiords or "sounds" that indent the eastern coast.

St. Lawrence Islands National Park

- **Province:** Ontario
- **Date Established:** 1914
- **Size:** 9 square kilometres (3.5 square miles)
- **Visits:** About 75,000 per year
- **Campgrounds:** Mainland campground provides 63 sites, and 15 island campgrounds provide additional 83 sites
- **Trails:** Day-use only

- **Local Communities:** Mallorytown, Lansdowne, and Gananoque
- **Access:** Via Thousand Island Parkway and boat from Mallorytown Landing
- **Contact:** Superintendent, St. Lawrence Islands National Park, 2 County Road 5, R.R. 3, Mallorytown Landing, Ontario K0E 1R0; telephone (613) 923-5261

With the help of a Parks Canada interpreter, the intertidal zone of Terra Nova National Park becomes a zone of discovery.

Terra Nova National Park takes its name from a river and a lake west of the park, and is Latin for "new land." It represents the Precambrian features and boreal forest of the Eastern Newfoundland Atlantic natural region of the national park system. The park's rolling hills are cloaked with black spruce and balsam fir, while wetlands are plentiful in the low-lying areas with vegetation such as mosses, orchids, and the insect-eating pitcher plant. Bogs and fens cover 15 percent of the park.

Separated from the mainland by the ocean, Terra Nova differs from other boreal forests in its wildlife. It includes native lynx, bear, and beaver, as well as introduced mammals such as snowshoe hare and moose. The park protects habitats for more than sixty-three nesting species, including bald eagle and osprey. In the coastal zone, where land meets sea, visitors can find sea urchins, starfish, mussels, periwinkles, and rock crabs. From shore, you can see whales and dolphins, which are attracted to the area by squid and caplin. Icebergs are also a common sight in late spring.

The idea of creating Newfoundland's first national park was first raised in 1947 when Newfoundland's entry into Confederation was being negotiated. In 1951 federal officials confirmed that the Bonavista Bay area represented the best coastal scenery in the province. The area eventually protected fell short of the federal government's hope to create a 1,000-square-kilometre (400-square-mile) park. Proposed boundaries were chipped away to exclude valuable timber and the Terra Nova River because of its hydroelectric potential.

Reminders of Terra Nova's cultural heritage lie along the park's coast. The earliest inhabitants, the Maritime Archaic Indians, took their food from the ocean and land nearly a thousand years ago. The Dorset Eskimos and later, the Beothucks, followed. Europeans reached the Terra Nova area as early as the 1500s. By the mid-1600s, the area was settled by the British, who developed the natural resources for logging, shipbuilding, and agriculture. Fishing and winter harvesting of wood for fuel and building remain important activities.

The integrity of park resources is threatened by commercial fishing, trapping, logging, and other developments of natural resources on lands adjacent to Terra Nova. Colonies of seabirds, such as common tern and eider duck, are also threatened by an increasing number of boats using coastal areas; the park is ideal for sailing and yachting. And pollution from offshore sources contaminates waterways entering the park.

The park has a strong emphasis on public education. It has six main interpretive themes: "Boreal Landscapes Touching Sheltered Seas"; "Climate"; "Ocean"; "Coastal Zone"; "Island Effect"; and "Perseverance of Man." The public can learn about the park's heritage resources at campfire talks, slide shows, illustrated talks, skits, kids' programs, guided walks, interpretive boat tours, and evening programs at two outdoor theatres.

Terra Nova National Park

- Province: Newfoundland
- Date Established: 1957
- Size: 400 square kilometres (154 square miles)
- Visits: Almost 200,000
- Campsites: 2 vehicle-accessible semi-serviced campgrounds providing 550 sites, plus 5 primitive campsites
- Trails: Almost 150 kilometres (90 miles) of hiking trails
- Local Communities: Charlottetown, Terra Nova, Eastport, Traytown
- Access: 222 kilometres (138 miles) north of St. John's via the Trans-Canada Highway on Bonavista Bay
- Contact: Superintendent, Terra Nova National Park, Glovertown, Newfoundland A0G 2L0; telephone (709) 533-2801

TUKTUT NOGAIT

Canada's newest national park, Tuktut Nogait, protects an arctic landscape of spectacular river canyons, abundant caribou and other northern species including muskox and wolves. Pronounced "Took-tut Nog-guide," the park name means "caribou calves" in the language of the Inuvialuit of the western Arctic. It was the Inuvialuit who first suggested creating this park, to help protect a caribou herd.

Located southeast of the community of Paulatuk and west of Coppermine, NWT, Tuktut Nogait is Canada's fifth largest national park at 16,340 square kilometres (6,310 square miles). Its two major conservation goals are to protect a representative portion of the Tundra Hills and to conserve the core calving grounds of the Bluenose caribou herd, which is culturally and economically important to the native people of the region.

The park's landscape is composed of tundra vegetation, rolling hills and deep river canyons. Visitors to this impressive new park can traverse one of the few areas to escape being covered by glaciers during the Wisconsin glaciation period; the higher elevation areas were a refugium for biota. Also found within the park are several steep-sided hills, called pingos, that have a core of ice buried beneath their surface.

The park's biodiversity is high for an arctic area due to the presence of a variety of micro habitats. Good nesting habitat is found in the park's abundant cliffs and ramparts along the Hornaday and Brock rivers. The density of nesting hawks, falcons and eagles is among the highest in the Northwest Territories. Excellent habitat for the region's barren ground caribou herd and muskox is found in the Melville Hills and its lush green valleys.

Plans for other national parks in this region were abandoned because of mining conflicts. Fortunately, the people of Paulatuk suggested the idea of creating a national park in 1989 after completing a community conservation plan that identified a national park as the best way to protect the Bluenose caribou herd. Seven years later, the final agreement creating the park was signed in Paulatuk, and passed into law by Parliament in 1998.

Parks Canada plans to expand the park into the traditional territory of the Inuit and the Sahtu Dene and Metis, thereby creating a park of over 28,000 square kilometres in size. Such a larger park would better represent the wilderness landscape of the Tundra Hills, and better conserve the calving grounds of the Bluenose caribou herd. Tuktut Nogait now gives people access to what author Ed Struzik calls one of "the great unexplored wildlands of mainland North America."

Tuktut Nogait National Park

- **Territory: Northwest Territories**
- **Date Established: 1998**
- **Size: 16,340 square kilometres**
- **Local Communities: Paulatuk, Inuvit**
- **Access: Dempster Highway or fly to Inuvik, then charter air to park, or boat from Paulatuk**
- **Contact: Superintendent, Box 1840, Inuvik, Northwest Territories, X0E 0T0, telephone (867) 777-3248**

VUNTUT

Located in the northern Yukon, Vuntut protects the Old Crow Flats, a vast plain of more than 2,000 shallow lakes and ponds. The Porcupine caribou herd, one of the world's largest remaining herds of barren-ground caribou, migrates through the Flats, which provide important fall, winter, and spring habitats. The Old Crow Flats are recognized as a wetland of international importance.

Vuntut National Park represents the vast interior plains of the Old Crow Flats in the Northern Yukon natural region. Along with Ivvavik National Park to the north, it encloses the key ecological features of this natural region that include wetlands, landforms, wildlife, and cultural resources. The area was withdrawn from any further industrial development in 1978 by the federal government following the recommendations of the Mackenzie Valley Pipeline Inquiry. There are no visitor facilities in Vuntut National Park.

In reaching a final land-claim agreement with Canada, the Vuntut Gwitchin Yukon First Nation agreed to the creation of Vuntut National Park. The Old Crow Flats remain central to the Vuntut Gwitchin people's culture and way of life. The native people and the federal government will manage this park cooperatively, emphasizing Vuntut Gwitchin history, culture, and use of the land, including harvesting rights.

The vegetation of the Old Crow Flats consists of a mosaic of wetland and aquatic species, along with cotton grass meadows and low shrubs on uplands. Old, gently rising hills called pediments form the landscape in the northern portion of the park. Underlain with permafrost, they support sedge tussocks, shrubs, and open stands of spruce and tundra. This is the northern limit of trees in Canada.

The Old Crow Flats are one of the most important waterfowl areas in the world. They support up to 300,000 waterfowl during breeding season, and up to half a million stage there in the fall. More than fifty-six sites of vertebrate fossils important for palaeo-ecological research have been found along the rivers that meander through the Flats. The artifacts found here provide evidence of very early human habitation and ancient animal species such as giant beavers and mammoths. Archaeological sites dating back almost 40,000 years provide evidence of human occupation of the Canadian north.

The Ivvavik-Vuntut national park complex, coupled with the adjacent Old Crow Flats Special Management Area, makes a significant international contribution to protecting the wilderness and wildlife resources

More than 2,000 shallow lakes and ponds are protected in Vuntut National Park.

shared by Canada and the United States in this region. The caribou with their new calves migrate in summer to the coastal plain of the Arctic National Wildlife Refuge and Ivvavik National Park in the northern Yukon.

To help create Vuntut National Park, six Canadian petroleum companies donated mineral permits covering more than 400,000 hectares (1 million acres) of Vuntut National Park to the Nature Conservancy of Canada, which in turn contributed the mineral interests to the federal government. The government had to acquire these permits before placing Vuntut National Park under the protection of the *National Parks Act*.

Vuntut National Park

- **Territory: Yukon**
- **Agreement in principle: 1993**
- **Size: 4,345 square kilometres (1,678 square miles)**
- **Facilities: None**
- **Local Community: Old Crow**

- **Access: Aircraft**
- **Contact: Superintendent, Vuntut National Park, Parks Canada, P.O. Box 390, Dawson City, Yukon Y0B 1G0; telephone (403) 993-5462**

WAPUSK

One of the world's largest and most southerly known polar bear denning habitats is now protected in Wapusk National Park, located south and east of Churchill, Manitoba. At 11,475 square kilometres, it is the largest national park located wholly within the provinces. The agreement creating Wapusk National Park was signed in 1996, and witnessed by HRH Prince of Wales.

Wapusk, pronounced "waa-pusk," is a Cree word for white bear. And the polar bear is the dominant wildlife species in this region. Every year, almost 10,000 people travel to Churchill to observe the polar bears. To escape the summer heat, polar bears construct summer dens to help them cool off, with some being six metres deep and hundreds of years old. As summer light fades to autumn, up to 120 bears will gather near Cape Churchill, waiting for the bay to freeze so that they travel on the ice.

The purpose of this, Canada's 37th national park, is to protect a portion of the Hudson-James Lowlands natural region of the national park system. This natural region is defined by its flat inland expanses of tundra, eskers and permafrost, and its proximity to Hudson and James bays. While discussions on this park were seriously initiated in 1989, the idea of a Churchill national park dates back to the early 1960s.

The lands and waters protected in Wapusk National Park are used by hundreds of thousands of waterfowl and shorebirds that nest along the Hudson Bay coast, or that migrate during annual spring and fall migrations. Its coastline is a bird watcher's paradise: lesser snow geese, small Canada geese, brant, whistling swans, oldsquaw, kind eider and northern phalarope, along with many shorebirds, all gather here in summer. Other wildlife species found in this park include caribou, moose wolves and wolverines.

Wapusk National Park

- **Province: Manitoba**
- **Date Established: 1996**
- **Size: 11,475 square kilometres**
- **Campgrounds: 1, including 550 sites**
- **Trails: Approximately 40 hiking and biking trails**

- **Local communities: Churchill**
- **Access: Highway 10 from Brandon or fly from Winnipeg to Churchill**
- **Contact: Superintendent, Box 127, Churchill, Manitoba, R0B 0E0, telephone (204) 848-7275**

Wapusk National Park was made possible because the Government of Manitoba was prepared to support the national park, but only if there was local support. Since the early 1990s, representatives of the community of Churchill and the First Nations of Fox Lake and York Factory have planned this new national park. The establishment of Wapusk National Park is the result of a consensus among the federal and Manitoba governments and local and Aboriginal communities, a consensus that serves as a model for future parks.

WATERTON LAKES

Waterton Lakes National Park marks a dramatic transition from rolling prairie grasslands to rugged mountains, giving rise to the park's interpretive theme "Where the Mountains Meet the Prairie." Located in southern Alberta, the park borders on the Continental Divide to the west, and the Canada–U.S. border and Glacier National Park in Montana to the south. In 1932 both Waterton Lakes and Glacier were declared an International Peace Park, the first in the world, recognizing that the natural character of this region is not severed by a political boundary.

The abrupt transition from the Prairie Grasslands natural region of the national park system to the Rocky Mountains natural region is represented in Waterton Lakes National Park. The result is that a very diverse natural environment is protected in one of the crown jewels of the national park system. Six major life zones have been identified in the park: wetland, prairie, aspen parkland, montane, subalpine, and alpine.

Indians called this area "Land of the Shining Mountains" long before the first Europeans arrived in 1800. Legend has it that the mountains, forests, and lakes of this region were created by Sokumapi, a fabled warrior. Fleeing from the Underworld with an Indian maiden, he cast aside a stick, and later a rock, creating a forest, and then a mountain, that slowed and eventually halted his pursuers. No longer needing a skin of mystic water, he emptied its contents alongside the mountains, creating the Kootenai Lakes, now known as Upper, Middle, and Lower Waterton Lakes. Geologists would probably tell a different story.

The idea for Waterton Lakes National Park was first suggested in 1883 by Frederick Godsal, a local rancher concerned that further settlement would erode the beauty of the region. In May 1895 the government created the Kootenai Lakes Forest Reserve by setting aside 140 square kilometres (56 square miles) of land. Development was not forbidden in the original reserve, and numerous boundary changes saw the park reduced to an area as small as 34 square kilometres (13.5 square miles) in 1911, and then expanded to its maximum size of 1,058 square kilometres (423 square miles).

Waterton Lakes National Park marks the western limit of the great Canadian plains. The fescue grassland protected in the park is among the most rare habitats conserved in the national park system. It provides important habitats for bison, coyotes, pocket gophers, and wildflowers such as lupine and shrubby cinquefoil. The lakes and ponds of the wetland zone support aquatic plants and ducks, geese, beaver, muskrat, and mink.

Groves of trembling aspen, which are characteristic of the parkland zone, are either surrounded by prairie grasslands or creep up into mountain valleys. The spruce, fir, and aspen forests of Waterton Lakes National Park, along with its prairie grasslands and alpine meadows, provide an important

Anderson Peak rises above Blakiston Valley. Lieutenant Thomas Blakiston is thought to have been the first European to set eyes on the region now partly enclosed within Waterton Lakes National Park.

habitat for plains bison, mule deer, moose, elk, grizzly and black bears, mountain goats, and bighorn sheep. And because the park is a transition zone from prairie to mountain, wildflowers from both regions are found here; for example, prairie rose grows near mountain fireweed. The park also protects over 110 species of Alberta's rarest flowering plants, 24 of which are not found anywhere else in the province. Bear grass is a lily that is found nowhere else in the national park system, and is the signature plant of the Waterton/Glacier International Peace Park.

Waterton Lakes National Park does not protect a complete ecosystem. Intensive land-use practices on surrounding lands are causing the loss of critical wildlife habitats and allowing increased access to the lands that buffer the national park from the impact of development. Some of the park's life zones are threatened by intensive recreational use of the main Waterton Lakes valley, the presence of exotic plant species such as spotted knapweed, the fact that the natural fire cycle is out of balance, and finally by growing pressure to sell adjoining ranchlands as real estate.

Waterton Lakes National Park

- **Province: Alberta**
- **Date Established: 1895**
- **Size: 505 square kilometres (195 square miles)**
- **Campgrounds: 3 campgrounds provide 391 sites plus 13 back-country campsites**
- **Trails: 255 kilometres (158 miles) of back-country trail**
- **Visitor Centre: Town of Waterton Park**
- **Local Communities: Cardston and Pincher Creek**
- **Access: 265 kilometres (164 miles) south of Calgary via highways 55 and 6**
- **Contact: Superintendent, Waterton Lakes National Park, Waterton Park, Alberta T0K 2M0; telephone (403) 859-2224**

WOOD BUFFALO

Open up a map of Canada and you can immediately spot Wood Buffalo National Park – a large chunk of green space that straddles the Alberta–Northwest Territories border. Parks Canada captures the tone of this park when describing its World Heritage features to Canadians: "It embodies those qualities of spaciousness and wilderness that symbolize the Canadian north and that are rapidly becoming precious world resources." Parks Canada has been challenged over the last several years by a number of proposed and existing developments inside and surrounding the park that threaten its future viability as Canada's largest national park.

Wood Buffalo National Park represents the ecological features of the Northern Boreal Plains natural region of the national park system. Four life zones are found here: the Alberta Plateau, the Slave River Lowlands, the Peace-Athabasca Delta, and the Caribou and Birch Uplands. The Alberta Plateau, which covers most of the park, contains meandering streams, shallow lakes, bogs, sinkholes, and large gypsum cliffs. The largest active gypsum karstland in the world is found here, where water has dissolved the gypsum bedrock, creating caves and tunnels, karst valleys or, where the surface collapses, sinkholes.

The Slave River Lowlands are located along the northeastern boundary of the park. Touching on the Canadian Shield, they mark the edge of the boreal plains, and here we find the Salt Plains, a 250-square-kilometre (100-square-mile) area that supports salt-tolerant plant species that are more common in maritime environments. There are also grassland and saline marshes that provide habitats for bison, waterfowl, and shorebirds. Underground water transports salt from beneath the surface, depositing it as either sheets or mounds.

In the southeast corner of the park is the 4,800-square-kilometre (1,920-square-mile) Peace-Athabasca Delta, containing shallow lakes, marshes, and grasslands that provide nesting, staging, and breeding areas for waterfowl. This spectacular natural feature is designated a world-class wetland, a Ramsar site, under an international conservation convention. More than 400,000 waterfowl use the delta during spring migration, in part

A white pelican on the Slave River, Wood Buffalo National Park.

because the delta provides a habitat for bird species that use all four major North American continental flyways that converge here. The delta has formed where the Peace and Athabasca, the two major rivers in the park, flow into the western end of Lake Athabasca.

In two small sections of the park, the Caribou and Birch mountains rise above the boreal plains to heights of more than 400 metres (1,312 feet). They are composed of sedimentary rock and have exposed fossils of great scientific interest. This area is practically inaccessible to visitors because the park is largely roadless.

This boreal wilderness is an important habitat for the largest free-roaming herd of bison in the world. The largest density of wolves in North America is protected in Wood Buffalo, producing a prey-predator relationship between wolves and bison that is both ecologically and behaviourally unique. And there are other reasons to treasure this large national park. For example, the park protects 80 percent of one of the world's largest freshwater deltas, the Peace-Athabasca. Prime bison habitat is provided by the largest undisturbed grass and sedge meadows remaining in North America. The park protects the last natural nesting grounds of the endangered whooping crane and the only breeding population of endangered peregrine falcons in southern Canada.

The park is named for its purpose: it was created in 1922 to protect the original habitat of wood buffalo in the vicinity of Fort Smith. The federal order creating the park concluded that, unless the area was protected, the only remaining wood buffalo herd in its native state could become extinct.

UNESCO added Wood Buffalo National Park to its List of World Heritage Sites in 1983 because the park protects significant natural phenomena and offers habitats where rare and endangered species still survive in a largely intact northern boreal ecosystem. Hard work has brought the whooping crane and peregrine falcon back from the edge of extinction.

In 1992 the federal court ended commercial logging in Wood Buffalo National Park because it was illegal under the *National Parks Act.* Logging was first permitted in 1956 as part of the federal government's plans to promote economic development in northern Canada.

Wood Buffalo National Park

- **Province/Territory:** Alberta/Northwest Territories
- **Date Established:** 1922
- **Size:** 44,802 square kilometres (17,299 square miles)
- **Visits:** About 9,000 per year
- **Campsites:** 1 serviced campground with 36 sites, 2 back-country campsites, and 1 back-country visitor cabin
- **Local Communities:** Fort Smith, Fort Chipewyan, Hay River, Fort Fitzgerald
- **Access:** By Mackenzie Highway system (Highway 35) and airports at Fort Smith and Fort Chipewyan. Highway 5 crosses park linking Fort Smith and Mackenzie Highway
- **Contact:** Superintendent, Wood Buffalo National Park, Box 750, Fort Smith, Northwest Territories X0E 0P0; telephone (403) 872-2349

Spiral tunnels were cut into the mountain on either side of Kicking Horse Valley to enable locomotives to negotiate the steep grades of the pass more easily and safely.

YOHO

Small wonder that Yoho National Park got its name from a Cree word meaning "wonder" or "excitement" or "awe." Glacier-fed waterfalls tumble off snow-capped mountains and quickly gather into roaring torrents. Two large icefields, Wapta and Waputik, envelop the Continental Divide, while an impressive range of peaks rises just to the west of the great divide. The Kicking Horse River valley cuts a wide swath through the park landscape, while most other valleys are narrow. Yoho Valley is the only vehicle-accessible of the narrow valleys with the road ending at Takakkaw Falls. Others are accessible by mountain-bike or hiking trails.

In 1886 the federal government laid the foundation for Yoho National Park when it reserved 26 square kilometres (10.4 square miles) around Mount Stephen. The exploration of the Yoho Valley by Dr. Jean Habel of Germany in 1896 brought the remarkable scenic attractions of the area to the attention of the government. In 1901 the reserve was enlarged to 2,153 square kilometres (861 square miles) and named Yoho Park Reserve.

Yoho National Park is the smallest of the four mountain parks (Jasper, Banff, Kootenay, and Yoho). It represents the western slopes of the Main Ranges in the Rocky Mountains natural region of the national park system. The headwaters of the Kicking Horse River, designated a Canadian Heritage River, are protected within the park. Because the Continental Divide wrings out the last bit of precipitation from the clouds that move east from the Pacific, the eastern limit of the interior western hemlock forest, western red cedar, and other species is reached in Yoho. And more than sixty mammal species are found in the park, including mountain goat, elk, white-tailed deer, and grizzly bear. It's more likely that visitors will see a moose or black bear, or even a coyote, than a grizzly bear.

Recreational use of Yoho National Park is heavy and concentrated around the back country of the Yoho Valley, Lake O'Hara, Emerald Lake, and the Trans-Canada Highway. Approximately 12 percent of the park is zoned for outdoor recreation, where human pressure on sensitive park resources is high. One of the popular features of the Yoho Valley is the waterfalls: Laughing Falls and Twin Falls, and Takakkaw Falls, one of Canada's highest waterfalls at 254 metres (833 feet). No wonder the park theme is "Rockwalls and Waterfalls."

The Burgess Shale, one of the world's most significant fossil beds, is protected in Yoho National Park. The shale contains the 530-million-year-old fossilized remains of more than 120 soft-bodied marine animals that were buried in an ancient sea. Author Stephen Jay Gould in his book *Wonderful Life: The Burgess Shale and the Nature of History* states that the Burgess Shale surpasses dinosaurs in its potential for telling us about life's history. Continuing research of the Burgess Shale has produced new ideas of the evolution of life on earth. The fossil beds were declared a World Heritage Site in 1981, and are closed to the public because they must be protected. Specimens can be seen at the Information Centre in Field. People who want to visit the site itself can join the park staff or licensed guides on hikes during the summer.

Yoho National Park reports a number of stresses on its heritage resources. Excessive use of the back-country areas is exceeding the environmental and social carrying capacity of places such as the Yoho Valley Wildlife mortality on the highways and railway tracks is a threat to wildlife populations. Sewage is polluting the Kicking Horse River. And elk, bear, and other species are being poached. Clear-cut logging and the development of roads on adjacent lands is encroaching on the park's natural buffer against development. This increasing insularization of Yoho National Park will lead to greater stress on some wildlife populations and communities.

Yoho National Park

- **Province: British Columbia**
- **Date Established: A small reserve was created in 1886, and later enlarged in 1901 and named Yoho Park Reserve.**
- **Size: 1,313 square kilometres (507 square miles)**
- **Visits: Over 700,000 per year**
- **Campsites: 4 road-accessible campgrounds provide 280 sites, plus 35 walk-in sites**
- **Trails: 360 kilometres (225 miles) of hiking trails plus horseback riding from stables at Emerald Lake**

- **Visitor Centre: Field**
- **Local Communities: Golden, B.C., Lake Louise and Banff, Alberta**
- **Access: 8 kilometres (5 miles) west of Lake Louise and 26 kilometres (16 miles) east of Golden, B.C., via the Trans-Canada Highway**
- **Contact: Superintendent, Yoho National Park, Box 99, Field, British Columbia, V0A 1G0; telephone (604) 343-6324**

THE NATIONAL PARKS AGENDA

"How can a minister stand up against the pressures of commercial interests who want to use the parks

for mining, forestry, for every kind of honky-tonk device known to man, unless the people who love these parks are prepared

to band together and support the minister by getting the facts out across the country?"

HON. ALVIN HAMILTON, MINISTER RESPONSIBLE FOR NATIONAL PARKS, 1960–1963

Cathedral Mountain in winter,

Yoho National Park.

Page 200:

The transition zone joining the southern

maple, birch, and beech forest, and the

northern spruce and fir, is clearly apparent

in La Mauricie National Park.

THE GLOBAL CONSERVATION AGENDA COMPELS CANADA TO EXPAND ITS NET-work of national parks. Under the terms of the *National Parks Act*, Parliament has a moral and legal obligation to maintain national parklands unimpaired for the benefit of future generations, and to give priority to the protection of natural resources over visitor use. The nation's commitment to imple-menting sustainable development requires that we ensure future generations have the same opportunity we have had to experience Canada's vast wild spaces and special natural areas. The following chapter outlines how we can live up to these obligations.

National Parks and the Human Potential

For many Canadians, encounters with national parks may consist only of glimpses of scenery beside the Trans-Canada Highway or brief strolls along interpretive trails. Over time, however, many people begin to demand more of themselves, and of the park system itself. Roadside stops no longer satisfy the soul as visitors search for the solitude that is one of the gifts of wild places. Leaving behind them the noise, pace, and clutter of our consumer society, visi-tors can explore the interior of a primeval forest, pause in the shadow of a mountain, or take shelter behind a sand dune as the waves crash on the beach.

Almost since the idea was first suggested, proponents of national parks emphasized that the focus should be on the experience of natural settings. This was suggested for various reasons: to rejuvenate the human spirit; to learn about nature; and to engage the contemplative faculties.

Perhaps Aldo Leopold said it best. In his classic book, *A Sand County Almanac*, he suggested that for national parks "recreational development is a job not of building roads into lovely country, but of building receptivity into the still unlovely human mind." The challenge is not to build a better road or facility but to lure people out of their cars, and encourage them to take a closer look at the infinite detail and variety in nature.

The renowned American architect Frederick Law Olmsted stressed in 1865 that the public interest in the Yosemite Valley rested "wholly in its natural scenery." He recommended the exclusion of all developments that would "obscure, destroy or detract from the dignity of the scenery." He warned that any "injury to the scenery so slight that it may be unheeded by any visitor now, will be one of deplorable magnitude when its effect upon each visitor's enjoyment is multiplied by these millions." Olmsted's advice was ignored; a century later the high level of tourism development in Yosemite is currently the most controversial issue in that park's management.

National parks offer visitors the opportunity to experience the awe-inspiring power of nature undistracted by the human activities and artifacts that increasingly dominate our lives. In essence, the task of park managers is to ensure that all visitors to a national park feel as if they are the first. To that end, the federal government's national parks policy attempts to minimize the number of facilities and attractions so that visitors are not distracted from the natural surroundings.

Environmentalists have lobbied for decades, with some success, for a national parks policy that promotes intensive *experience* rather than intensive use. It is the outstanding views, the encounters with wildlife, and the pleasant fatigue following a long day's hike or paddle, that give satisfaction. This is a change for us in a world where the intensive use of natural resources is more often correlated to a healthy national economy. Our enjoyment is related less to how many miles we drive or hike, or how many photographs we take, or how many birds we add to our life list, than to the experience itself.

In national parks, visitors can observe how species have adapted and grown in a variety of environments. We look with awe at centuries-old Douglas fir trees. We marvel at the colourful flowers that bloom in a seemingly hostile environment. We stare for hours at waterfalls that have discharged water every second for hundreds of years. Nature is also a model of the many things we value in human communities: continuity, stability, and sustenance. One can see in undisturbed natural settings many examples of architecture, food production, resistance to disease, energy use, and conservation. This is the practical value of studying the diversity of life that is retained in national parks: nature provides ideas and materials for energy efficiency medicines, and new foods.

Behind every national park, and each scene within it, there is a story.

There is the natural history of an area — how a valley was shaped by glaciers, how the mountains were created, how the forest evolved, and how it supported the evolution of life. And there is human history — of the Haida of Gwaii Haanas and the Inuvialuit of Ivvavik, of the explorers and railwaymen in Rogers Pass, and of century-old fishing villages in Gros Morne and Forillon. They help us understand how previous generations perceived, used, and exploited or protected the Canadian landscape and all its native wildlife.

National parks are an invitation to present generations to explore, discover, and understand the roots of natural and human history. But through them we also pass on to future generations wild landscapes that represent the diversity of the natural world out of which we forged Canadian society. We are also passing on a source of ecological knowledge that may be critical to the resolution of the ecological crises in the future.

THE FADING WILDERNESS

Our ability to pass on a legacy of wild places is challenged by the extent to which human activities are altering the life-sustaining processes of the planet. Virtually no place on earth is free of human impact. This was brought home in 1993 when scientists found traces of industrial pollutants and car emissions around the South Pole. Even this, perhaps the last pristine area on the planet, is tainted by human activities. We can no longer assume that our wilderness areas will survive unimpaired, whether or not they are protected. This situation has clear implications for our national parks.

A growing number of studies indicate that Canada's national parks and protected areas are under stress from human activities. Opportunities to preserve more wilderness areas are diminishing because wilderness is disappearing at the rate of one square kilometre (a half square mile) per hour. Viable wilderness areas larger than 50,000 hectares (125,000 acres) no longer exist in much of southern Canada. The natural areas adjacent to national parklands are also being developed, often with dire consequences for the parks themselves. The following vignettes illustrate the types of problems that confront park planners and environmentalists.

■ Plans for a national park in the Gulf Islands of British Columbia have sat on the shelf for decades. Opportunities to protect one of Canada's most diverse natural regions within the national park system were promising in the 1970s. Work has only seriously begun in the past few years, however, and development in the same period has narrowed options for a national park down to a few remnant natural areas.

■ The boundaries of Riding Mountain National Park are clearly visible in photographs taken from space. Forests on all sides of the park have been cleared for agriculture, making Riding Mountain an ecological island in a sea of farmland. Black bears, ignorant of the manmade park boundary, suffer a high death rate on adjacent lands from hunting and other activities.

■ Wood Buffalo is Canada's largest national park. It's the size of Switzerland, but even this massive boreal wilderness is buckling under development pressure. The expansion of logging operations and pulp mills outside the park, the construction of an upstream dam on the Peace River, and proposals to eliminate the park's diseased bison herd all threaten this World Heritage Site. The World Conservation Union commented in 1991 that the park's large size is "no longer an adequate basis to ensure its long-term integrity."

■ Woodland caribou are declining in Pukaskwa; piping plover nests are threatened in Kejimkujik; exotic species are replacing native species in Grasslands; airborne pollutants are degrading the atmosphere over Ellesmere Island; and logging up to the boundaries of Prince Albert, Pukaskwa, La Mauricie and Fundy national parks is having a major impact on park ecosystems and wildlife habitat.

■ Today Banff townsite is more an icon to commercialization than a shrine to the birthplace of Canada's national parks. Hotels, convention facilities, shopping malls, downhill ski areas, all supported by an expanded highway network, continue to consume parkland, and to distract visitors from the essential conservation message of Banff National Park.

These are not isolated cases. They are symptoms of the problems that confront our century-old national park system. In 1994, Parks Canada summarized trends across the park system after having identified the significant ecological stresses on 34 of Canada's national parks. Among its findings:

■ Eleven percent of all reported significant ecological impacts on national parks originate from within park boundaries, 36 percent originate totally from external sources, and 53 percent of all stresses occur without regard to parks boundaries.

■ Forty-three percent of the 34 national parks report that the significant ecological stresses on their parks are increasing, while 12 percent report that they are decreasing, with the remaining stresses either stable or an unknown trend.

■ The impact of forestry operations outside 18 national parks was the most ferquently reported external source of stress on park resources, with agriculture (15 parks), sport hunting (13 parks), and mining (10 parks) the next most reported stresses.

■ The most reported significant ecological impact on park ecosystems was caused by the construction and operation of visitor and tourism facilities located both inside and outside national parks.

National parks are often described as the nation's crown jewels. But remove the crown and you are left with a loose collection of coloured stones whose

Visitors of all ages enjoy a walk along the intertidal zone of Pacific Rim National Park Reserve.

value is greatly diminished. In developing the land around national parks and reducing them to isolated ecological islands, we are destroying the crown that supports these wilderness jewels.

One place where this is painfully obvious is an area called the Crown of the Continent ecosystem, encompassing the southwest corner of Alberta, the southeast corner of British Columbia, and northern Montana. Canada's Waterton Lakes National Park and Glacier National Park in the United States protect the core wilderness of this region. But it is not enough. Oil and gas developments, cattle grazing, recreational developments, and logging are all encroaching on the park boundaries. Grizzly bears that wander in and out of the park are continually at risk because they are shot, poisoned, or trapped and removed to other locations. Naturalist Kevin Van Tighen writes that those who control the Crown of the Continent often "view it as real estate and resources, to be fought over, parcelled out, then exploited – rather than as a unique ecosystem to be treated humbly with respect."

As the growing number of external threats to national parks clearly reveals, parks are not fortresses with solid walls that prevent pollutants from entering, or wildlife from leaving. Rather, park limits act as permeable membranes through which acid rain, toxic chemicals, exotic species, and pesticides pass freely. Park boundaries also signal a change in administration. Inside national parks the federal government has jurisdiction over the resources, but outside it is virtually powerless to affect land-use practices. So even if a superintendent knows about activities outside the park, he may lack the power, or the backing of his political masters, to stop the damage to park resources.

The problem becomes more critical as the parks become more isolated within the larger terrain. Park boundaries that originally existed only on maps are now clearly visible to the human eye. The loss of natural buffers is isolating the parks with damaging consequences. But lands and waters that are critical to park ecosystems extend well beyond park boundaries. Development in park buffer zones reduces and destroys critical wildlife habitats used by park wildlife, and the quality and quantity of water that crosses into park boundaries. For example, no complete ecosystems or watersheds remain intact within the Long Beach and West Coast Trail areas of Pacific Rim National Park.

Construction of the Bennett Dam on the Peace River in British Columbia offers a dramatic example of how development can adversely affect park resources. While the dam is hundreds of kilometres upstream, it reduced spring flooding of the Peace-Athabasca Delta in Wood Buffalo National Park because the dam captured and retained the runoff. The result is that the prime bison habitat is now changing from high-protein sedges to indigestible silverweeds and thistles. In addition, pollution from upstream pulp mills in Alberta is depositing toxic chemicals in the shallow, slow-moving waters of the delta. Pregnant women and native elders are now warned to lower their consumption of fish taken from the delta.

Each year more than sixteen million people visit the national parks for a typical Canadian holiday. But the arrival of thousands of cars, trailers, and tents, and the physical impact of millions of boot-shod feet, are having a negative impact. The sheer number of people is stressing some environments, and ruining the wilderness experience that back-country users are seeking. More than 500 tonnes of garbage are trucked out of Yoho National Park annually to landfill sites near Calgary at a cost of thousands of dollars each year. So many people have taken to hiking the West Coast Trail in Pacific Rim National Park Reserve that you now have to reserve a place months in advance.

The federal government devotes a substantial part of the national parks budget to providing visitor facilities. Roads, parking lots, hydro and water corridors, washrooms, showers, golf courses, hotels, warden cabins, boardwalks, hiking and biking trails, visitor centres, rescue and medical facilities are all part of the business of running and maintaining a national park.

Park managers now identify tourism infrastructure as the most common stress on park resources. The preoccupation with visitor services has resulted in a national parks program where engineers can tell you about the "health" of the park infrastructure, but ecologists can only guess at the "health" of the park ecosystem. While this is slowly changing, a greater portion of the national parks budget continues to be spent on facility development and maintenance than on conservation.

THE CONSERVATION AGENDA FOR OUR NATIONAL PARKS

Decisions made in this decade will largely determine the size and health of the national park system that future generations will inherit. The Canadian

The pitcher plant traps insects for food, Terra Nova National Park.

Environmental Advisory Council produced "A Protected Areas Vision for Canada" in 1991 that elaborates on the decisions required. It recommended that Parks Canada:

■ complete its network of national parks representing each of the federal government's thirty-nine natural regions by the year 2000;

■ manage each national park on an ecosystem basis, meeting compatible social and economic needs on adjacent lands, while maintaining the park itself in as natural a state as possible; and

■ enhance educational and interpretive programs in national parks so that natural heritage values become part of a nationally unifying environmental ethic.

The Council's vision is that national parks "will become catalysts for the improved management of human activities in all parts of Canada and ... for improved global environmental management."

What does it mean to "complete" the national park system?

Before 1970, the national park system was a system in name only. It was a loose collection of parks promoted by a visionary few. Parks had been established for a variety of different reasons: to promote regional development through tourism, protect scenery, or conserve wildlife habitats. In the late 1960s, partly in response to public pressure to protect the environment, several Liberal cabinet ministers in charge of national parks suggested the creation of forty to sixty new parks. Given the growing pressures for more national parks, Parks Canada needed a guiding ecological principle on which to base system expansion.

The principle chosen, described in an earlier chapter, was to preserve samples of all Canada's landscapes. To date, twenty-four of the thirty-nine natural regions are represented within the national park system. There are gaps in Labrador, Quebec, Manitoba, British Columbia, Yukon, and the Northwest Territories. The government has a stated goal of establishing at least sixteen additional parks to represent the remaining natural regions by the year 2000. There are three basic steps to achieving this goal: identify candidate sites; conclude negotiations for their protection with provincial and territorial governments, aboriginal people, and local communities; and protect them under the *National Parks Act*.

What does it mean to manage the national parks on an "ecosystem" basis?

National park managers must work more closely with land owners and development interests that surround national parks to ensure that park ecosystems are protected. Scientists are now trying to define the "greater park ecosystems" that must be conserved outside park boundaries. The goal is to manage the national park as an integral part of the landscape. This entails management of human activities on a regional scale so that the protected area values are maintained while accommodating human interests and economic activities on adjacent lands.

The short-term goal of greater park ecosystem projects is to identify the external and internal stresses on park resources, and to work to reduce and eliminate them. In a 1992 government survey of park managers, the most commonly reported sources of negative effects on national parks included tourism and park infrastructure, exotic vegetation, utility corridors, commercial forestry, acid rain, agriculture, urbanization, and hydro dams. Restoration of park ecosystems is also a short-term priority. Water levels in a number of national parks, such as Prince Albert, have been artificially raised, changing the nature of aquatic ecosystems. Several parks are reviewing conservation data to see if they should remove some restrictions to water flow, which could affect canoeing opportunities.

The long-term goal is to protect enough habitats within and outside national parks to ensure that all native species, including wide-ranging grizzly bears and wolves, survive. This will require all land mangers to establish long-term goals to ensure that enough land is protected for centuries to allow species and ecosystems to evolve in relatively undisturbed natural areas. However, such conservation efforts must allow for human use and occupancy at levels that do not result in significant ecological degradation of greater park ecosystems. This, of course, does not mean that parks should be opened to industrial and increased tourism development.

To set long-term goals for the management of the ecosystems that surround national parks and protected areas forces us to confront several issues. We need to establish a comprehensive understanding of the ecological relationships among the various plants, animals, and natural features that form an ecosystem. At present we are relatively ignorant of how ecosystems function. In addition, we need to assess the cumulative impact of developments on regional ecosystems and park resources. For example, an assessment of the cumulative impact of all the tourism development in the four mountain parks is required before any further development can be permitted.

We are also confronted with the philosophical question that is asked more and more these days: Do we give priority to exploiting and developing natural resources for human benefit, or do we give priority to saving nature? In drawing park boundaries, and permitting the continued development of park ecosystems for tourism inside the national parks and for other activities outside, we have consistently favoured the former. The government has been working to protect most national parkland in a wilderness state. But the declining quality of park resources clearly suggests that we need to give priority to saving nature.

FROM VISIONS TO CONSERVATION GAINS

Apart from a few halfhearted attempts, the federal government has rarely demonstrated a sustained commitment to expanding the national parks system. The minister of national parks told Parliament in 1930, "It is our hope that eventually there will be a national park in each province of the Dominion." This goal was not achieved until Forillon became Quebec's first national park in 1969. In 1967 the Liberal government suggested completing the national park system by 1985, which marked the centennial of the first national park. But by 1985, the system was only half complete.

After World Wildlife Fund (Canada) launched the Endangered Spaces campaign in 1989, Canadians from coast to coast voiced their support for completion of the national park system by the year 2000. When it was released in December 1990, the federal Green Plan made a formal commitment to achieve the goal. Prime Minister Jean Chrétien vowed to "maintain the commitment to complete the National Parks System by 2000" during both of his successful election campaigns.

Since the release of the Green Plan, four new national parks were created, protecting over 44,000 square kilometres of wilderness. An additional four candidate areas, totalling over 66,000 square kilometres, were given interim protection until park negotiations are complete. Following are some of the sites that may soon become part of the national park system.

NATURAL REGION 2 — STRAIT OF GEORGIA LOWLANDS

Tucked under the rainshadow of Vancouver Island's mountains, this natural region has a balmy Mediterranean climate. Warm dry summers, mild winters, and a cluster of islands amidst a fertile sea all combine to produce natural habitats found nowhere else in Canada. The Gulf Islands, with forests of Douglas fir, western red cedar and lodgepole pine, along with pockets of rare Gary oak savanna, are home to many rare and endangered species. Since this is the smallest and most urbanized natural region of the national park system, it is difficult to find a large undisturbed site for a national park. Much of the area has been logged or farmed, and fast-paced urban development is foreclosing what conservation options remain.

The federal and British Columbia governments launched the Pacific Marine Heritage Legacy program in 1995 to acquire lands for a new national park and provincial protected areas in the Southern Gulf Islands. Thirteen properties totaling 1,032 hectares had been acquired by April 1998 at a cost of $24 million. They include Bodega Ridge, whose cliffs provide habitat for bald eagles and peregrine falcons; Tumbo Island, a largely forested island with old-growth Douglas fir trees and one of the finest remaining stands of Garry oak and arbutus parkland; and the Mill Farm Property on Salt Spring Island, which includes one of the largest remaining stands of old-growth Douglas Fir in the southern Gulf Islands.

NATURAL REGION 3 — CHURN CREEK AREA

The Churn Creek area in the Chilcotin plateau region of British Columbia varies dramatically from the semi-desert grasslands and rugged canyons of the Fraser and Chilcotin rivers, through expansive old-growth Douglas fir and ponderosa pine forests and upland meadows, to alpine tundra in the Coast Range. Rich in biodiversity, the area supports an abundance of wildlife, including North America's largest herd of California bighorn sheep, cougar, bobcat, grizzly bear, wolverine, moose, and ptarmignan. The diversity of landscapes offers world-class river rafting, spectacular wildlife viewing opportunities, and hiking and horseback riding.

Plans for a Churn Creek national park in this area were greeted with lukewarm public support. Fortunately, the creation of two provincial protected areas, plus the acquisition of the grasslands in the Empire Valley Ranch, have resulted in the protection of 1,027 square kilometres. Perhaps public support for a national park here will emerge over time, and this nationally significant landscape will become one of the jewels of the national park system.

NATURAL REGION 14 — MANITOBA LOWLANDS

The heart of the proposed Manitoba Lowlands national park is two natural areas: a 1,489 square kilometre core around Long Point encompassing the lands between lakes Winnipeg and Winnipegosis; and a 1,352 square kilometre unit to the north focused around Limestone Bay. The Long Point area is one of the larger undeveloped wilderness and biologically diverse landscapes in the Lowlands, containing a mix of upland and lowland topography and associated wetlands, the Pas Moraine, beaches and sand dunes, and major staging areas for waterfowls and shorebirds during spring migration. The Limestone Bay area contains one hibernation site for Little Brown bats, important spawning habitat for walleye, escarpment cliffs and one of the longest spits in Canada.

NATURAL REGION 16 — CENTRAL TUNDRA REGION

Wager Bay in the Northwest Territories is an inland sea that extends more than 150 kilometres (90 miles) from the western coast of Hudson Bay and includes 8-metre (26-foot) tides, a reversing falls, and diverse marine wildlife. The landscape varies from rocky bluffs on the southwest shore to rolling hills, shallows, and low-lying islands in the northwest. Prehistoric stone remains are still in evidence along the rocky shore, left by the Inuit who used these lands as far back as 4,000 years ago. The narrows at both ends of Wager Bay create tidal currents strong enough to keep stretches of water free of ice all winter, forming "polynias" – winter havens for marine mammals and seabirds.

This proposed park has been dormant for almost two decades because of the lack of community support. However, with the settlement of the Inuit land claim in 1993, interested communities have entered into formal negotiations with Parks Canada towards establishing a Wager Bay national park. In October 1996, Prime Minister Chrétien announced the interim protection of 23,600 square kilometres pending the outcome of negotiations with the Inuit. Long-term prospects for Wager Bay becoming a national park are more promising than ever.

NATURAL REGION 17 — NORTHWESTERN BOREAL UPLANDS

The East Arm of Great Slave Lake candidate site straddles the tree line with vegetation ranging from boreal forest to open tundra. It includes a large peninsula and some islands on Great Slave Lake, Northwest Territories. Five ecological regions occur over a remarkably short distance within this proposed park. Rugged cuestas and high cliffs of the peninsulas in Great Slave Lake contrast with the more subdued terrain of the tundra around Lac la Prise and Artillery Lake. Large eskers, reminders of the last ice age, snake across the tundra landscape.

Over 7,400 square kilometres (2,960 square miles) were withdrawn from development in 1970, but despite several attempts the park proposal has not been advanced because of a lack of local community support. Unfortunately, Tyrell Falls on the Lockhart River, located in the heart of the proposed park, was left outside the withdrawal because of its hydroelectric power potential; it is critical that it be added to the park. The future of this national park proposal will depend on the support of the Aboriginal people in Lutselk'e. Until then, the site is protected from the mining fever that has gripped the region.

Natural Region 21 — Mealy Mountains

Rising steeply from Lake Melville, the Mealy Mountains are the easternmost extension of the Canadian Shield. Because tree cover is sparse, they stand out as a large island of Arctic tundra in southern Labrador. The proposed park includes a mix of boreal forest, mountain tundra, and marine ecosystems. One of the last roadless expanses of boreal forest in North America, it includes extensive sand beaches, bogs, lakes and wild rivers with spectacular waterfalls. The proposal is home to a dwindling herd of barren-ground caribou, moose, black bears, wolves and a variety of smaller mammals. More than 140 bird species, including the bald eagle and rough-legged hawk, are found here. The endangered eastern Harlequin duck also breeds in the area.

A Mealy Mountain national park was first proposed in the early 1970s. While Parks Canada and the Innu Nation, who have an unsettled land claim to the area, are prepared to advance the park proposal, the Government of Newfoundland and Labrador has placed its priority on developing the natural resources of the larger region. Thus, the ecological integrity of any future national park is increasingly compromised, as plans for forestry, road construction, hydroelectric power development and mineral exploration are advanced. This conservation initiative is needed to offset the impact of growing development in southern Labrador.

Natural Region 22 — Boreal Lake Plateau

Located 100 kilometres (60 miles) north of the Great Whale River, the Lac Guillaume-Delisle proposed national park is a remote and pristine wilderness. The Riviere à l'Eau-Claire is the backbone of this candidate park, with its headwaters originating in Quebec's second-largest natural lake, Lac à l'Eau-Claire. The river flows west over a number of large, cascading waterfalls to Lac Guillaume-Delisle, a vast brackish estuary linked to Hudson Bay. The Quebec government confirmed this area as a potential provincial park in 1992, and withdrew the land from development pending further study. The candidate site is located within the territory covered by the James Bay and Northern Quebec agreement, which guarantees the participation of native people in the management and development of the territory. The next step is for the governments of Canada and Quebec and the organizations representing aboriginal interests to initiate a park feasibility study.

Natural Region 24 — Torngat Mountains

The proposed Torngat Mountains national park in northern Labrador encompasses a true Arctic landscape that includes impressive fiords and the highest, most rugged mountains east of the Canadian Rockies. A spectacular wilderness environment, its fiords cut inland up to 80 kilometres, and its cliffs rise sharply from the sea up to a kilometre in height. Polar bears roam the coast, while the George River caribou herd, the world's largest at 700,000 animals, ranges through the proposed park. The proposed park encompasses one-third of the traditional homelands of the Labrador Inuit, who support the creation of Labrador's first national park.

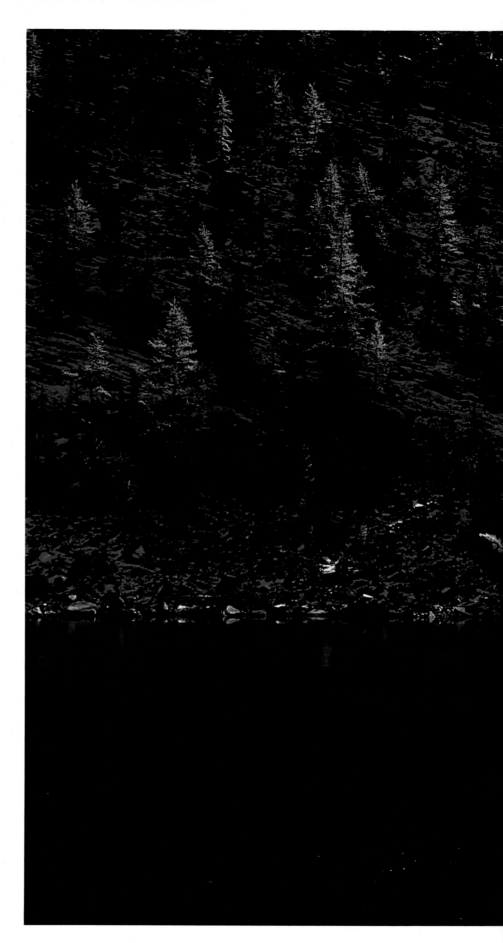

Banff, Canada's oldest national park, continues to be among the parks that are most heavily used by visitors.

Environmental groups hope that once the national park is established it will include the Ramah Bay area to the southeast. Currently outside the proposed park because of its mineral potential, it contains vital calving grounds for the smaller Torngat caribou herd; the most northerly breeding and nesting area of the endangered Harlequin duck; and habitat for the globally unique population of tundra-dwelling black bears. There is no question that the Torngat Mountains will become a national park; the unanswered questions are when, and what the final boundaries will be.

Parks Canada has also identified two new candidate sites: in 1995, it launched a study to determine the feasibility of a national park on Northern Bathurst Island in the Northwest Territories; and in 1998, it identified the Wolf Lake area in the southern Yukon as a candidate park. About 8,700 square kilometres of land are temporarily protected on Bathurst Island pending the outcome of study, providing interim protection to the endangered Peary caribou. The initial Wolf Lake proposal is over 16,000 square kilometres, approximating the home-range of a resident woodland caribou herd. Decisions on these two sites will be several years in the making.

The job of identifying and negotiating new national parks rests with the Park Establishment Branch of Parks Canada; the job of actually establishing these new parks rests with federal politicians. Politicians, however, are not compelled by law to protect more wilderness areas or to establish new national parks. Only public pressure compels them to act. Both political will and public agitation were required to save the South Moresby wilderness.

In 1987, members of Parliament of all political stripes rose in the House of Commons and called for the preservation of the South Moresby wilderness. Environment Minister Tom McMillan acknowledged "the strong hold that that unique collection of islands has exerted in the consciousness

of Canadians." New Democratic Party environment critic Jim Fulton pointed out that "over 3.5 million people represented by various groups have petitioned the Government of Canada…asking that the area be set aside as a national park reserve." McMillan recalled how he had received over a thousand personal letters in three months, including one from an eleven-year-old Cape Breton boy who told him, "It's not good enough to just talk. You have to do something." During this debate on May 14, 1987, Parliament unanimously resolved to create a national park reserve on the Queen Charlotte Islands. That goal was achieved only two months later.

The historic parliamentary debate demonstrates that Canadians must inform their political representatives through letters, phone calls, and meetings that they want action on wilderness protection. A clear indication of public support for proposed national parks must be aimed directly, clearly, and often to politicians of all political persuasions. Without public support, the penchant of politicians is to force park proponents to respond to every conceivable issue raised by their opponents, and to allow candidate national parklands to be allocated to development, hectare by hectare.

The federal government must secure the agreement of three separate parties before it can create a national park: the provincial governments who administer all Crown land south of the Yukon and Northwest Territories; aboriginal organizations who have unresolved title issues or treaties covering lands that are potential national parks; and local communities that could benefit, or be affected, by the proposed park.

Negotiations can fail for a number of reasons. Governments may be unwilling to forgo the development opportunities afforded by the exploitation of the area's natural resources. Land may have already been allocated for logging, mining, oil and gas, or other developments. Outstanding aboriginal land claims and unresolved title issues could also hamper negotiations.

And local communities may conclude that the proposed national park would have a negative impact on their way of life.

However, these obstacles are slowly falling. There are active park candidates in over half of the unrepresented natural regions. Aboriginal people have become more supportive of the national park concept. The extractive industry supports the completion of representative protected area networks, which include the national park system, through mining and forestry accords with environmental and aboriginal groups. And the federal government is more active in securing the interim protection of candidate sites until planning is complete.

Negotiations with the Quebec government, however, could be difficult because of its long-standing policy against the transfer of lands to the federal Crown for national park purposes. (Forillon is a ninety-nine-year lease agreement; La Mauricie was created as part of a federal-provincial land swap; and the Mingan Archipelago was purchased from Dome Petroleum.) Negotiations are also complicated by on-again, off-again constitutional discussions. However, both governments have agreed upon some sites for park status, raising the potential for joint protection measures.

Aboriginal people have demonstrated a growing interest in new national parks once they are assured there will be action on unresolved land claims, and that they will have a role in managing park resources. The last four national parks, Aulavik, Vuntut, Wapusk and Tuktut Nogait, were created mainly because of aboriginal support. The Nunavut final agreement commits the federal government to representing each of the natural regions in Nunavut in the national park system. And the Labrador Inuit are willing to set aside one-third of their homeland in Torngat Mountain national park.

Many aboriginal leaders have said they are willing to share their land with Canadians. But it must be on their terms, respecting their interests and

aspirations, which include hunting to sustain their people, and job opportunities. The national parks system has greatly benefited from the support
of native people and land-claim settlements in the past two decades. Success
in expanding the park system depends on the ability of the government and
aboriginal leaders to agree. Negotiations for virtually every future national
park will involve native people.

Local communities have also shown a willingness to embrace new
national parks. In 1990, for example, the Inuvialuit of the community of
Paulautuk identified protection of the Bluenose herd of 115,000 barren-
ground caribou as a priority in their community conservation plan, and a
national park as the means to achieve this goal.

The challenge is to convince local communities that the natural
wonders around them are less a commodity to exploit than a treasure to
preserve, and to demonstrate that national parks can assist in providing
tangible environmental, social, and economic benefits. Establishing new
national parks in rural areas brings park supporters face to face with the fears,
frustrations, and aspirations of people increasingly alienated from a society
that is 90 percent urban based. It is a challenge that we must succeed at
because national parklands will survive over the long term only if there is
community support for the natural values they protect. If not, pressure for
more development both within the park and on adjacent lands will ultimately
lead to their demise.

Maintaining the National Parks Unimpaired

Point Pelee National Park is Canada's second-smallest national park. Its natural
environment has a long history of human manipulation. Trapping, agriculture,
mining, and oil and gas exploration occurred before the park was created in
1918. After it became a national park, there was extensive recreational use and
development in the park including roads, cottages, duck hunting, and the
removal of underbrush to make the park more appealing to visitors.

Point Pelee was one of the more abused national parks in the past.
The priority now is to restore and protect this unique Carolinian ecosystem,
and its vulnerable native plants and animal species. This requires reducing
the impact of the over 500,000 annual visitors; removing the exotic plant
and animal species that are out-competing native species; reintroducing
some species, such as the southern flying squirrel, that are locally extinct;
and trying to achieve more compatible land-use practices outside the park.

The changes that have been effected are remarkable. Camping is no
longer permitted. Cottaging is almost completely phased out. Duck hunting ended in 1988 and the East Beach road was removed in 1990. To protect
the sensitive vegetation on the sand dunes, you can get to the beach only
by crossing boardwalks. An over-abundant population of deer, grazing on
endangered plant vegetation, was recently culled. The movements of snakes
are being radio-tracked to determine which habitats should be more strictly
conserved. These advances are inspiring. If one of Canada's smallest, most
affected national parks can demonstrate progress in conserving an endangered ecosystem, there is hope for others.

If park values are to survive, then Parks Canada must gain the support
of adjacent landowners and other interests that operate within park ecosystems. The Crown of the Continent Society is one initiative that has brought
industry, environmentalists, hunters, ranchers, governments, and tourism
interests together to help plan a future for the ecosystem surrounding
Waterton Lakes National Park. This mix of interests produced a common
vision for the Crown ecosystem: "To guarantee to future generations of all
living things a masterpiece of nature, known as the Crown of the Continent,
through a locally based cooperative approach which will ensure the preser-

Lake McArthur, Yoho National Park.

vation, wise use and restoration of the natural environment and the well-being of area communities." The hope is that the society will achieve a lasting commitment to the natural values of the Crown ecosystem and its core protected area, Waterton Lakes National Park.

Perhaps we are witness to a transition — a shift from dominant industrial values to an appreciation of the natural values of this region. Several years ago, Hilton Pharis, then chairman of the Crown of the Continent Society and a local rancher, remarked that all the development pressures in the region "could erode the natural values we grew up with here." He believed that through the Society "we have to convince people and governments to take the hard decisions to protect [the area's] integrity, and that sometimes means saying no to development." Whether the Society will make a real difference remains to be seen, but it is a start.

In defending national park values, conservation groups and the federal government sometimes find themselves at odds. Industrial logging in Wood Buffalo National Park was ended in 1992 only after the government was sued by the Canadian Parks and Wilderness Society and the Sierra Legal Defense Fund for breaching the *National Parks Act*. Recent decisions by the federal government to expand the Trans-Canada Highway through Banff National Park, and to permit further expansion of the Sunshine Village ski facility, have provoked opposition from environmental groups because of the increasing pressure these and other developments are placing on the natural values of Canada's first national park.

It was these threats that led the Liberal government to appoint the independent Banff-Bow Valley Task Force in 1994 to provide direction on the management of human use in Banff. Their conclusion was unmistakable: "The current rates of growth in visitor numbers and development, if allowed to continue, will cause serious, and irreversible, harm to Banff National

Park's ecological integrity." In a new park management plan, the Liberal government took several important steps to limiting and removing development. But it has yet to embrace completely the bold steps recommended by the Task Force; much more is needed if Banff is to survive the coming decades.

For many years national parks were created chiefly as a reaction to the threat of development. It was assumed that by drawing an artificial boundary, we could protect special natural features from the ravages of industrial society. We now know that proposition to be flawed. The enduring legacy of Sir John A. Macdonald's farsighted action in 1885 is a patchwork of protected places in which we can develop a new appreciation and understanding of nature. Our task now is to look beyond park boundaries, and to apply the same level of care and respect to the entire Canadian landscape. We have only one natural home. It's time we treated it as home.

The CPR started to make hiking trails in the Valley
of Ten Peaks, Banff National Park, in the early 1900s.

Kayaking may be the ideal way to explore the islands in the Mingan Archipelago for those who possess the skills and the proper equipment.

How You Can Help

To learn more about the need to protect Canada's wilderness lands, get a copy of *Protecting Canada's Endangered Spaces: An Owner's Manual*, edited by Monte Hummel (Toronto: Key Porter Books Limited, 1995). This collection of essays explains in detail the work needed to complete a network of protected areas across Canada. The Canadian Nature Federation is a partner in the Endangered Species campaign with its focus on securing federal action to complete the national park system by the year 2000. *A Citizen's Action Guide to Completing the National Park System* is available from the Canadian Nature Federation.

Go to the Source!

The best way to learn about national parks is to visit them. Experience at first hand the natural areas that represent the diversity of the Canadian landscape. When you arrive, acquaint yourself with the park by stopping at the Visitor Centre. Take an interpretive walk to learn about the park's distinctive life zones. And visit the retail outlet operated by the local Cooperating Association, such as the Friends of Yoho or Friends of Point Pelee, where you can purchase a number of items that support conservation programs in the park, and help you learn about parks and the environment.

For additional information on how the natural resources of a particular park are conserved, write to the park and ask for a summary copy of the park management plan.

Speak Up!

The federal government is responsible both for creating new national parks and ensuring the preservation of existing parks. There are various representatives of the government, including the federal minister in charge of national parks, your local member of Parliament, and the park superintendent, to whom you can express your views.

Write to them to express your support for a proposed national park, opposition to the continuing loss of national parklands to development, or concern about a particular issue in a national park you are familiar with or have visited. Ask for a response, and if you are not satisfied, write again.

But write! Your letter may lend support to ministers and civil servants who are trying to create new parks and protect existing ones. And if you don't express your view, chances are those seeking to exploit our parks and wilderness areas will win the day. *Don't let your member of Parliament off the hook. He or she has a responsibility to ensure our national parks are passed on to future generations unimpaired. It is the law!*

Write to the Minister of Canadian Heritage, House of Commons, Ottawa, Ontario, K1A 0A6. Check the blue pages at the back of your phone book to find the phone number for your local member of Parliament, and phone to get his or her name and address. Addresses for park superintendents are found in the park descriptions in this book.

JOIN UP!

Join a conservation group that works to create new national parks and to preserve existing national parks from inappropriate development. These national, provincial, and local conservation groups work hard to convince politicians, civil servants, and all Canadians of the need to conserve more wilderness land and to maintain it for future generations. The more Canadians support these groups, the more effective their public advocacy and education programs.

Through their magazines and newsletters, these conservation groups keep you informed about the value of national parks. They also track the various threats to the national parks, and identify opportunities for Canadians to write letters about a particular issue. Two of the groups working on national park issues are:

Canadian Nature Federation
1 Nicholas Street, Suite 606
Ottawa, Ontario, K1N 7B7
(613) 562-3447

Canadian Parks and Wilderness Society
401 Richmond Street West, Suite 380
Toronto, Ontario, M5V 3A8
(416) 979-2720

These two organizations can supply you with the addresses of provincial and local conservation groups working to protect Canada's national parks.

DONATE MONEY

If you want to make a financial contribution to the cause, there are a number of worthy organizations to which you can donate money.

You can support World Wildlife Fund's Endangered Spaces campaign to represent each of Canada's 486 natural regions within a national network of parks and protected areas. Contact World Wildlife Fund, 90 Eglinton Avenue East, Suite 504, Toronto, Ontario M4P 2Z7.

The Nature Conservancy of Canada also helps to support the expansion of the national park system and to conserve important natural areas across Canada. Contact Nature Conservancy of Canada, 110 Eglinton Avenue West, 4th Floor, Toronto, Ontario M4R 2G5.

The Canadian Nature Federation, working with the Nature Conservancy, has established the Grasslands Trust Fund to help acquire land for the yet-to-be-completed Grasslands National Park. Contact the Canadian Nature Federation, 1 Nicholas Street, Suite 606, Ottawa, Ontario K1N 7B7. Each of these groups will provide you with a receipt for your charitable donation, which is tax deductible. Inquire about the availability of gift certificates to use as a Christmas or birthday gift. Give the gift of conservation!

The view from the summit in the Kluane Range of the St. Elias Mountains.

PHOTOGRAPHIC CREDITS

All photographs are by J.A. Kraulis unless otherwise indicated.

Mike Beedell: 17, 65, 92, 94, 112, 117, 172, 174, 219

Mike Beedell / Parks Canada: 124

Claude Bouchard: 22, 91, 95

Pauline Brunner: 19

Ralph Brunner: 108, 113, 115, 116

T.W. Hall / Parks Canada: 160, 162

Wayne Lynch: 74, 135, 136

Wayne Lynch / Masterfile: 179

Wayne Lynch / Parks Canada: 132, 144, 147, 152, 171, 196, 207

P. McCloskey / Parks Canada: 206

S. Mackenzie / Parks Canada: 190

Kevin McNamee: 161

Pat Morrow: 75, 111, 114, 153

Brian Milne / First Light Associated Photographers: 73, 146

Parks Canada: 126, 134, 137, 140, 143, 145, 156, 170, 178, 180, 183, 186, 188, 192, 198

P. St-Jacques / Parks Canada: 166, 168

J. Stevens / Parks Canada: 158

Ed Struzik: 120

John de Visser: 189

Darwin Wiggett / First Light Associated Photographers: 71, 72, 133

SELECTED BIBLIOGRAPHY

Berger, Thomas R. *Northern Frontier, Northern Homeland.* Vancouver: Douglas and McIntyre, 1977.

Brown, Robert Craig. "The Doctrine of Usefulness: Natural Resources and National Park Policy in Canada, 1887-1914." In J.G. Nelson, editor. *Canadian Parks in Perspective.* Montreal Harvest House Limited, 1969.

Canada. Minister of Supply and Services. *State of the Parks Report,* Volume 2: *1990 Profiles.* Ottawa, 1991.

Catlin, George. "An Artist Proposes a National Park." In Roderick Nash, editor. *The American Environment.* Don Mills, Ontario: Addison Wesley Publishing Company, 1976.

Chrétien, Hon. Jean. "Foreword." In John Theberge, editor. *Kluane: Pinnacle of the Yukon.* Toronto: Doubleday Canada Limited, 1980.

Foster, Janet. *Working for Wildlife: The Beginning of Preservation in Canada.* Toronto: University of Toronto Press, 1978.

Henderson, Gavin. "The Role of the Public." In J.G. Nelson, editor. *Canadian Parks in Perspective.* Montreal: Harvest House Limited, 1969.

IUCN. "Monitoring the State of Conservation of Natural World Heritage Properties." Report prepared by IUCN for the World Heritage Committee meeting in Carthage, Tunisia, December 9-13, 1991.

Leopold, Aldo. *A Sand County Almanac.* New York: Ballantine Books, 1966.

Lopez, Barry. *Arctic Dreams.* Toronto: Collier Macmillan, 1986.

Lothian, W.F. *A Brief History of Canada's National Parks.* Ottawa: Minister of Supply and Services, 1987.

Marcia, Kaye. "Pick Me! Pick Me!" *Canadian Living.* Vol. 18, No. 9, September 1993.

Marty, Sid. *A Grand and Fabulous Notion: The First Century of Canada's Parks.* Toronto: NC Press Limited, 1984.

Nash, Roderick. "Wilderness and Man in North America." In J.G. Nelson and R.C. Scace, editors. *The Canadian National Parks: Today and Tomorrow.* Calgary: University of Calgary, 1969.

Page, Robert. *Northern Development: The Canadian Dilemma.* Toronto: McClelland and Stewart, 1986.

Rowe, Stan. *Home Place: Essays on Ecology.* Edmonton: NuWest Publishers Limited, 1990.

Runte, Alfred. Yosemite: *The Embattled Wilderness.* Omaha: University of Nebraska Press, 1990.

St-Amour, Maxime. *Forillon National Park.* Vancouver: Douglas and McIntyre, 1985.

Stephenson, Marylee. *Canada's National Parks: A Visitor's Guide.* Scarborough, Ontario: Prentice-Hall Canada Inc, 1991.

Van Tighen, Kevin. "Waterton: Crown of the Continent." *Borealis.* Vol. 2, No. 1, 1990.

Waiser, Bill. *Saskatchewan's Playground: A History of Prince Albert National Park.* Saskatoon: Fifth House Publishers, 1989.

Wareham, Bill. *British Columbia Wildlife Viewing Guide.* Edmonton Lone Pine Publishing, 1991.

Woodcock, George. *The Century that Made Us: Canada 1814-1914.* Toronto Oxford University Press, 1989.